# Woman, TRASHED

# Woman, TRASHED

*Joanne Brodie*

PENGUIN BOOKS

PENGUIN BOOKS

Published By the Penguin Group
Penguin Books (South Africa) (Pty) Ltd, 24 Sturdee Avenue, Rosebank, Johannesburg 2196, South Africa
Penguin Books Ltd, 80 Strand, London WC2R 0RL, England
Penguin Group (USA) Inc, 375 Hudson Street, New York, New York 10014, USA
Penguin Group (Canada), 90 Eglinton Avenue East, Suite 700, Toronto, Ontario, M4P 2Y3, Canada (a division of Pearson Penguin Canada Inc.)
Penguin Ireland, 25 St Stephen's Green, Dublin 2, Ireland (a division of Penguin Books Ltd)
Penguin Group (Australia), 250 Camberwell Road, Camberwell, Victoria 3124, Australia (a division of Pearson Australia Group Pty Ltd)
Penguin Books India Pvt Ltd, 11 Community Centre, Panchsheel Park, New Delhi – 110 017, India
Penguin Group (NZ), 67 Apollo Drive, Mairangi Bay, Auckland 1310, New Zealand (a division of Pearson New Zealand Ltd)

Penguin Books (South Africa) (Pty) Ltd, Registered Offices:
24 Sturdee Avenue, Rosebank, Johannesburg 2196, South Africa

www.penguinbooks.co.za

First published by Penguin Books (South Africa) (Pty) Ltd 2009
Reprinted 2010



ISBN 9780143026105

Typeset by Nix Design in 12/14pt Lapidary
Cover design by Minette de Villiers
Printed and bound by Interpak Books, Pietermaritzburg

*For Darren, my son and soulmate,*
*and Ca, my sister and earth angel*

# Prologue

It was 2002 and I was just over eight years clean. I had recently left the addiction treatment centre where I'd been head of counselling to go into full-time private practice. Finding the right venue for my practice had proved to be quite difficult, until one day I'd discovered Bella Vita.

Bella Vita was, amongst other things, a Reiki centre. Although I had never before heard of this universal method of healing through energy, I soon found myself undergoing individual sessions and becoming an ardent student of the practice. I loved it. I loved how it was changing me – I felt softer, somehow. Transformed.

But the sessions revealed something besides my new sense of self. Patricia, my practitioner, later told me she'd sensed something amiss; there'd been moments during our sessions when I'd become agitated and distressed. But she'd trusted that whatever was wrong would come out when the time was right.

Nothing could prepare me for when it did.

It began as an ordinary session a few months after my arrival at the centre. That morning, instead of the usual relaxing calm, I started to feel incredibly uncomfortable. My body ached all over and I became ice cold, colder than I'd ever felt before. And nauseous. For a moment, I considered asking Patricia to stop the session, but by then I was deep in meditation, and the thought quickly drifted away.

I began to become aware of a strange, disturbing image flickering in and out of my consciousness. At first the vision was disjointed and vague, but after a while I realised that what I was seeing was a baby. Not some generic infant, though. It was me as a small baby girl.

I began to identify other images; a cot, a familiar blanket. Harmless objects, yet for some reason they evoked in me a claustrophobic terror. Something was horribly wrong with this scene.

It was then that I saw him, and realised what was happening to this baby – to me.

For the next few weeks I walked around in a permanent state of nausea and numbness. As time went on, I relived shocking violations, obscenities infinitely painful to recall. And over and over in those early days of revelation I would find myself repeating, 'Now I understand. Oh, okay, now I understand'. The years of self-destruction, the incomprehensible torment I'd suffered all my life, finally made sense. What I didn't know then was that the nightmare wasn't quite over. I had yet to acknowledge the full truth of what had happened to me.

# 1

## Jo Jo the fatty

It was one of those sweltering hot January afternoons in the days when we still had summers. I could feel the sweat forming on the back of my thighs as I sat on the front porch reading. It was too hot to concentrate. I put the book down and went to find my mother in the lounge.

She was standing to one side, making certain that the tables and chairs were set up to perfection for her bridge party.

'Can I have some money?' I asked her.

'What for?' she asked, a tight expression on her face. I sensed something was bothering her.

'Ice cream.'

She frowned. 'I'm sorry, Jo Jo,' (how I hated that nickname; it sounded so round and childish), 'but Johnnie and I have decided we're not going to give you money for sweets anymore. We think it's time you started watching your weight.' Johnnie was my stepfather.

He'd married my mother six years after my parents' divorce.

I felt myself growing warm. The heat started at my toes and kept climbing all the way to my crimson-flushed face. Familiar voices started up in my head, repeating themselves, 'You see, Joanne, you're fat. Fat fatty fat. You're a fat, ugly pig!' Over and over the voices went. Hot tears stung my eyes as I stood facing her, humiliated.

I realise now that she only meant to help. Admittedly, at eleven I had acquired some puppy fat. But her implication that the extra weight was my fault, for wanting to buy and eat sweets which I had never been denied before, made me feel guilty and ashamed.

And so I became a secret eater. I started hiding candy, chocolates, chips and anything else that I thought was verboten in the drawer next to my bed, tucking into them in private and discarding the wrappers under my bed. At night or when my parents were out I would raid the pantry – although it was kept locked, I always knew where the key was. The most sought-after loot was jelly powder, condensed milk and Zoo biscuits, which I would eat very slowly, carefully licking the icing off each delicious biscuit. I would also plunder the sweet cupboard for chunks of caramel fudge and Callard & Bowser nougat to soothe my young proverbial hole in the soul. I must have been on an almost permanent sugar high, especially since the energy wasn't being utilised for any physical exertion – the only exercise I got was walking to the corner café every day.

Some time later, I gained a co-conspirator, Elly, who would accompany me on these daily trips to the café. One day we were on our way to stock up on our favourites of the moment – bright red cherry lollypops, six at a time, thick brown toffee and Beechies Mellofruit chewing gum. Ambling home with packets of contraband and eating liquorice en route (a daring feat for me because eating in public was an admission that food actually passed my lips), we spotted Dani walking towards us.

Dani was two years older than us, slim and sexy with thick blonde hair that tumbled down her face and shoulders in a golden veil. She was quite irresistible, all the boys adored her. I hated her.

Never mind green, I was positively jaundiced with jealousy.

And we were about to run into her not only with our mouths full but with brown paper packets containing our damning evidence. What to do? Elly and I looked at each other and it was one of those moments when words were unnecessary. We knew. We threw our offending packets of shame over the nearest wall into some unsuspecting person's garden. As we came closer to the goddess, I sucked in my breath and contracted my tummy as far as I could. Unfortunately this meant that I was unable to breathe, so it didn't stay flat for long. Our paths crossed. We mumbled hello. And that was that. She was gone.

Of course we were immediately sorry we had ditched our stash, but there was no way we could get it back, and we were left feeling deflated and as bad about ourselves as before – just hungrier. United in our shared humiliation, Elly and I silently agreed never to discuss this incident, and the next day we were back at the café.

For years this secretive eating continued, in between guilt at what I was doing and frequent though usually unsuccessful attempts at losing weight. In my family you could never be too thin or too rich. As a child, I could hardly be expected to contribute to the family's wealth, but clearly I disappointed them by not being able to control my weight. I felt so bad about this that I even blamed my weight for my parents' divorce, believing my father had left us because I was too fat. To me it seemed like everyone in the family was perfect but me.

My sister Carolyn, or Ca, was six and a half years older and everything I wasn't; slender, with clear golden skin and glossy hair, self-assured and attractive. She also had an offbeat sense of humour and an impressive ability to put people at ease, which made her popular. Handsome and charming, my brother Richard was a chip off the old block. Everyone said he looked like my father, who was often compared to Sean Connery. By the age of thirteen the girls were already throwing themselves at his feet. My mother, Dee, was as beautiful and elegant as Grace Kelly. And as popular.

And then there was me, awkward, clumsy Jo Jo, with the mousy brown hair and the pigeon toes which had prevented me from pursuing ballet. Sometimes I'd fantasise I was a foundling child, that one day I'd be claimed by my real family who would take me in and love me unconditionally. I remember the first time I had that fantasy; it was during one of my father's rare visits to South Africa after the divorce, when I was about ten or eleven. After my parents split, and after some dubious business dealings, he left South Africa and made his way to the South of Spain, followed by his girlfriend (part of the reason for the divorce). Here he had gone on to produce three more sons, whom us children referred to rather unkindly as the Spanish pigs. There was a little girl as well, but sadly she died soon after birth. After fathering this progeny, my father quickly abandoned them and their mother in hot pursuit of Sophie, who was my sister's age, and moved to London. Sophie was gorgeous, an ex-model, though not the sharpest knife in the drawer. But then my father had always preferred 'pretty poppies'. I can only speculate that intelligent women made him feel less powerful.

That night we were meeting him at Connoisseurs, one of Joburg's fashionable restaurants. I recall how on arrival he scanned the crowded restaurant looking for our table. The expression on his face when he glanced first at Ca then Richard was a mixture of pride and satisfaction. And then he looked my way.

What I saw on his face could only be described as disappointment. It was at that moment that something inside me shifted. Nothing had been said, but the rejection in that look was harsher than any words. My heart and chest felt so tight and sore that I forgot to breathe as I struggled to hold back the tears. Everything hurt, even my stomach. But I would not allow him the satisfaction of seeing my pain.

Instead, I looked down at my plate and willed myself to think about the family that would save me one day; the father who would admire my intellectual abilities, the mother who would tell me every day how beautiful I was, a swan in her eyes.

But as the night went on and I sat there listening to my father asking Richard about his rugby, chuckling at news of his escapades, and teasing my sister about her latest admirer, I could no longer deny it; I wanted to be loved by this man. I yearned for him to accept me.

At one point, during a lull in the conversation, I asked him a question about London. I don't remember his answer, only the way he had looked over my shoulder as he spoke, avoiding eye contact.

I couldn't understand why he treated me this way. I presumed it was because I wasn't good enough, because I couldn't possibly measure up to my illustrious siblings. That night, I decided I would never again allow myself to be called Jo Jo. And I would do everything I could to avoid feeling the way I had in that restaurant – hurt, rejected and humiliated.

Little did I know the lengths I'd go to to do this.

# 2

# High school and other highs

It was 1968, the year of revolution. While John Lennon chanted, 'You say you want a revolution. Well, you know, we all want to change the world,' in Paris, workers and students barricaded the streets in protest against the 'old society'. Even here in apartheid South Africa the hippy culture was pushing its psychedelic tentacles through cracks in the Nationalist government's fortress. I was twelve going on thirteen, and experiencing a revolution of my own.

One Saturday afternoon, at our home in Melrose North, I was about to smoke my first joint with Blondboy. I had met Blondboy at a 'social' a few weeks before. He was good-looking and, most appealing of all, quite a lot older than me. I certainly wasn't about to let on that this was my first exposure to Mary Jane. When he came over that afternoon to suggest we smoke some weed, I agreed with the nonchalant calm of a seasoned dope smoker. Absurd, considering my age, but then I was well practised at pretending.

'So where shall we do it?' he asked.

'Ag, wherever. My parents are out, so we don't have to hide. Let's just do it here.' We were standing in the driveway.

He shook his head. 'No, they might come back early. Let's find somewhere more private.'

'What about the rose garden? I suggested. 'You can see the front gate from there.'

He agreed, and we settled down on the grass beside the rose beds, partially hidden by the bushes. I was excited to be so close to him, doing something so forbidden.

I watched, fascinated, as he took out the paraphernalia – the Rizla, the bank-bag containing the weed – and began rolling the joint. What would it taste like? I wondered. How would it feel? Impatiently, I sucked on a Dunhill, another newly acquired vice, which had the advantage of making me look older and more experienced than I was.

At last Blondboy finished preparing this totem of my initiation and lit up. After drawing heavily, he offered the joint to me. Solemnly, with a certain amount of reverence, and trying to look like this was something I did all the time, I took a deep drag. By then it was a bit soggy. Yuck! I felt it burn my throat and a cough threatened to reveal my amateur status, but miraculously I managed to keep it at bay. 'Christ, this tastes revolting!' I thought to myself, passing it back to Blondboy.

By the time we finished the joint he was really out of it, red-eyed and giggling constantly for no reason. I, on the other hand, was completely sober.

'So how do you feel?' he asked, grinning.

'Bombed,' I lied. 'Hey, why don't we smoke another one before my parents get back?' I said. He laughed at my enthusiasm.

'Yeah, why not?'

The next joint took forever to roll, but this time it hit my brain and I was officially trashed. I didn't like it, though. It made me feel depressed and I was already well acquainted with that mood. It also gave me the 'munchies' in a big way, and God knows I didn't need more food in my life. But while I didn't enjoy the weed, and would never really smoke it much after those initial few months, what I did enjoy, loved, in fact, was having an altered sense of reality.

My thirteenth year had been a difficult one. I had started at a new high school down the road, a government school. It wasn't a bad place; it was just very different from Redhill, the private school I'd been to before. Also, all my friends had gone to different schools or stayed on at Redhill, while at the new school everyone seemed to know one another from their primary schools and soon formed cosy cliques of friends. I really struggled in the beginning. The bell would ring signalling break and I wouldn't know what to do. I felt embarrassed and would slink around feeling rather like a leper. It didn't help that I was also really self-conscious about my weight. Every now and then, I would tentatively approach a few of the girls, praying that I wouldn't be rejected. I was on edge constantly, and couldn't wait for break to be over.

At home I was feeling more alone than ever. Richard had moved out, and my mother, Johnnie and Ca were preoccupied with the new baby. I'd never seen anything as gorgeous as my brother Phil, and I loved him to bits, but a one-year old was hardly much company for a troubled teen.

Discovering drugs ameliorated my feelings of being an outsider and offered a welcome respite from loneliness. The confidence I gained from taking drugs and identifying myself as a user enabled me to break into one of the cliques and feel accepted. At first I mainly smoked weed, and then later that year I discovered the cough mixture Phensedyl. Phensedyl contained both codeine and ephedrine so it offered a double whammy. Codeine is one of the alkaloids of opium but twice as strong, and ephedrine is a stimulant. The word 'codeine' comes from the Greek word kodeia, which means 'poppy head'. I was delighted to be a poppy head. After all, how could anything that sounded so cute and pretty be harmful? I didn't know that the ancient Egyptians had recorded the paradoxical nature of opium in their medical texts, listing it as a cure for all illnesses, a pleasure-inducing substance, and also a poison. Not that the bit about poison would have put me off. I was hooked immediately and in no time I went from tentative sipping to glugging down a whole bottle fairly quickly. The great thing about Phensedyl, apart from the way it made you feel, was that it was legal. I could cruise into any pharmacy and purchase my magic potion without invoking suspicion. In those days, pharmacists did not suspect someone my age to be a serious dope-fiend in the making.

By the end of Standard six I'd established a small group of close friends. The highlight of my week was Saturday, when we would all descend on downtown Johannesburg to take in a movie at His Majesty's Theatre, one of the renowned cinema houses of the day. In between lunch and the film, I would swig back my cough mixture and then sit on the floor right in front of the screen. Being high certainly enhanced the silver-screen offerings of the day. I wanted everyone to know I was using and I perceived that my eccentric behaviour proclaimed my drug-taking status to all. Fortunately for my young self, perception is king, because looking back, I blush that I made such a spectacle of myself.

Despite my self-consciousness, I craved attention, and if being a rebellious and weird teenage junkie was the way to command it, I would go to extraordinary lengths in pursuit of this prize. None of my girlfriends were really interested in taking drugs; some flirted sporadically with them, but most were content to live vicariously through me, and I was happy to oblige.

The Woodstock festival in 1969 made me feel excited and excluded at the same time. I waited for the film version in great anticipation, and when it finally reached our shores, I was one of the first to watch it. Naturally I was trashed at the time, and thrilled to be part of a worldwide phenomenon, albeit from the floor of the theatre. If most of my life was imperfect, Woodstock symbolised my idea of perfection and affirmed my lifestyle choices. Already then I could not picture a life without chemicals and struggled to understand why anyone would want to go through life 'straight'.

At that stage I considered Timothy Leary a god and 'Turn on, tune in and drop out' became my mantra. Ironically, though, I only ever took hallucinogens once. But considering that experience it's not surprising I never did them again.

It happened one evening at my friend Jillian's house, during one of her frequent get-togethers. Jillian and I had an unlikely friendship. She was gorgeous. With her pale blonde hair she looked a little like a white tiger and she had the most beautiful blue eyes I have ever seen. She was refreshingly unaware of her incredible good looks, which made her more human and less intimidating for me.

She was one of the few friends I had who shared my love for mood-altering substances, and it was through her that I was first introduced to the merry world of Old Brown Sherry. On the nights that she stayed over at my house, we would spend hours playing klabberjas – a card game played in Jewish communities worldwide, and in itself hugely addictive. Our libation during this card marathon was Sedgwick's Old Brown Sherry, which quickly became my nectar of choice. Cloyingly sweet, it produced a rosy glow which seemed to enhance the game.

I loved playing cards, and we were like trained gladiators, tireless in our dedication to the game. We would sit, practically glued to my bed, fags hanging out our mouths, at all times single-minded in our focus on the all-important game. We were as earnest in our dedication as two old men playing boules. It seemed like such innocent fun but, in retrospect, I can see my obsessions were already hard at work building on and adding to existing patterns. Our chain-smoking was so intense that I'm surprised we didn't expire from the lack of oxygen in the confined space of my bedroom. We became such inveterate gamesters that, no longer content to play only outside school hours, we started playing at break-times, luring a few of our other cronies into our klabberjas web.

On the night in question, Jillian and her invitees had smoked a bit of weed. Due to my issues around dope, I declined to partake but helped myself to sherry and some tired looking nuts and raisins. There was no other food on offer. Feeling mellow, I looked around and saw some brown creepy things that looked like tumours lying casually on a plate. Not that I'd ever seen a tumour before, but I imagined they'd look something like what was on that plate. I asked the girl next to me, 'What the hell are these?'

'Magic mushrooms,' was her response. Naturally, I had heard of magic mushrooms, but I didn't believe they were available in South Africa. Convinced of my superior knowledge, I thought to myself, 'Yeah right!' Nevertheless, I picked up a few of the shrivelled, mouldy things, stuck them in my mouth, chewed and swallowed them. In my wildest flights of fancy, I could never have conceived of what came next.

The twelve hours that followed my sampling of these innocuous-tasting fungi became my personal Armageddon as I fought for my sanity. Within about thirty minutes, I began hallucinating and was officially 'tripping'. Maybe I would have freaked out and had a bad trip anyway, but because I wasn't expecting the mushrooms to be psychoactive, I was not primed for the experience. I became extremely anxious and kept repeating, 'I can't come down; I can't come down!' in mounting hysteria.

My reality, distorted to begin with, morphed into a paranoid parody of Fantasia, replete with ominous fairies and grotesquely large flowers and leaves that were menacing in the extreme. I had seen the re-release of this Disney film a few months previously and, contrary to popular and fashionable opinion, had loathed it. It made me very uncomfortable; perhaps it had offered a portent of what was yet to come.

My senses were confused. Walls were melting and lurid, noisy colours dripped everywhere. I could hear them waxing lyrical from the centre of the universe. Sounds oscillated from nowhere in particular, dancing triangularly down staircases. Outside my body now, I kept trying to be 'normal' and okay, but it was impossible. I had absolutely lost control of what was happening to me, at me and with me, and was sure that death was imminent.

'Jill, I think I'm losing it,' I moaned. 'You won't believe what I'm seeing, it's crazy! I feel like I'm in a nightmare. You have to help me!

'God, Jo!' Jillian's eyes were wild with anxiety compounded by the weed she'd smoked. 'I don't know what to do!'

She looked around her in the vain hope that someone else would know what to do, but the others were just as stoned and helpless.

'Um, why don't you lie down for a bit?' she pulled me onto a nearby couch, chucking empty coats and bags and cigarette packets onto the floor, and helped me onto it like an invalid.

Just then her older sister came home with her boyfriend, a doctor, in tow. Excited and relieved, Jillian briefed them on my situation and begged the doctor boyfriend for help.

'You have to do something!' she implored. 'She said she feels like she's dying! I don't know what to do. Please help us!' By now she was close to frantic.

'You fucking little punks!' was his terse response. 'What the hell are you doing messing around with this shit?' And with that he promptly left, declining to become involved in this messy drama. I can't say I blamed him.

So I remained on the couch in a semi-catatonic space for what seemed like years until about twelve hours later I felt myself returning to my senses. Clearly the stuff wasn't completely out of my system, though, as I recall how on the walk home I felt as if I were taking giant bounds and that I arrived at my house within seconds.

After that experience, chemically and energetically depleted, I suffered a katzenjammer of note. I love that word; it sounds like what it is; a mother of a hangover. This misadventure reinforced my fear of hallucinogens and I continued to resist any and all future acid or mushroom invitations. But even though I had experienced a frightening trip, at least it wasn't what we called the 'far trip', a journey from which there was no return. I knew a few people who had ended up in mental institutions permanently from experimenting with 1960s psychedelics.

Around the time of Woodstock, I inadvertently crossed a Rubicon in terms of my career as a drug addict when I was introduced to serious but legal amphetamines in the form of oblong, banana-coloured appetite suppressants called Obex. Ever on a crusade to control my offending and burgeoning weight, my mother conspired with our local and friendly doctor, and I was prescribed 'redemption in yellow'. This doctor, by now a family friend, considering how much time he spent with us, would become one of my 'dealers of choice', as he was always happy to provide me with a prescription for various and sundry tablets in exchange for a few 'innocent' pats on the bum.

The new pills took my using to new heights, literally as well as figuratively. I would pop one of these babies in the morning before school, and for the first part of the day, would feel fabulous, quite euphoric. Anything and everything seemed possible and all self-doubt was banished. Sadly, by afternoon I would crash, my mood plunging into hopeless despair. At which point I would seek solace in my sweet addiction. Naturally, I would feel even more hideous after bingeing, but then the next morning I'd rediscover salvation in my regular dose of speed. The popular slogan of the day, 'Better living through chemistry', epitomised not only me but also my family, wherein the dictum was 'A pill for everything' – including emotional maladies. We were a pharmacist's dream.

Needless to say, both my mother and father were addicts. In blissful ignorance of her enslavement, my mother, a staunch Valium enthusiast, could have been a character out of Jacqueline Susann's *Valley of the Dolls*. Cushioned by a lifetime of denial, she would probably rise from her grave in hearing herself labelled an addict. Sorry, Ma! Nevertheless, her bathroom cabinet was filled with row upon row of what the Rolling Stones coined 'Mother's Little Helpers' – pills bearing the brand names of the day, Valium, Librium and Halcion, to name but a few.

My father cultivated his alcoholism over the years but because he wasn't a fall-down drunk he got away with being classified as a 'functional alcoholic'. For my money, he was a raging dipsomaniac in denial as well as the quintessential sex and love addict, long before there was any such label or diagnosis. He defined himself by his many trophy women, and for years I would meet middle-aged women who, on hearing that I was Mervyn's daughter, would delicately blush and tell me somewhat breathlessly, 'I knew your father.' Hmm, indeed, and no doubt in the biblical sense, were my less than charitable thoughts.

In my case, the magnetism towards chemicals was so instant and immediate that I am convinced not only that my addiction was hereditary but also that I was habituated long before I picked up my first drug. I know that I would have been a druggie regardless of when and where I started. I was a walking time bomb, just waiting for the hidden code to trigger self-destruction; it was simply a matter of time.

The Obex and I became fast friends and it was a relationship that would certainly stay the distance, for better and worse. I developed tolerance quite quickly and increased the recommended dosage only to experience that the initial feelings of well-being and confidence diminished over time and transformed into irritability and paranoia.

But despite these unpleasant side effects, I was like a converted zealot, swallowing this amphetamine congener ritualistically every morning. Long after the drugs stopped working, I continued my self-limiting behaviour; such is the power of addiction. I was too scared to stop taking the drug as the consequences of abstinence proved shattering. On the few occasions that I went without my daily dose, I felt listless and depressed, and entertained constant thoughts of killing myself.

Did I lose weight? Not really. Once my system became accustomed to the substance I held onto the vain hope that it would be a miracle cure. Alas, like all instant gratifications, it was temporary at best, though I remained eternally optimistic about its magical properties and like an alchemist waited for myself to be transmuted into the golden girl, whippet thin and desirable.

I manifested another compulsion in adolescence that was every bit as, if not more, addictive than my chemical use. Certainly it was my biggest secret, which for me, the Queen of Secrets, says a great deal about its nature. Unaware that my behaviour had been shaped by sexual abuse, this new compulsion reinforced my self-perception that I was the most perverse and sickest person on the planet. I am referring here to masturbation. Even writing the word brings up shame; it is an ugly word, the etymology of which explains the negative energy that surrounds it. One of the suggestions is that it derives from the Latin manus, meaning hand, and stuprare, meaning defile.

The other theories around its derivation are equally indicting, bearing connotations of bad, dirty and unacceptable. Other words like self-stimulation or self-pleasure, however, seem inadequate to convey the act and are too politically correct for my liking. I have thus accepted that 'masturbate' captures its essence sufficiently to override my personal distaste.

The gaps in my memory dictate that I don't remember exactly when I developed this 'secret weapon', a non-chemical quick fix, but it was some time in the midst of my chaotic teenage years. One afternoon I discovered a stash of *Playboy*, *Penthouse* and *Mayfair* magazines next to my stepfather's bed. At once shocked and intrigued, I felt driven, perhaps by an unconscious internal narrative, to take a peek. After that first glimpse I found I wanted to see more. This proved to be fairly challenging as my mother was usually at home and spent time 'resting' in her room most afternoons. Patient and already well skilled at stealth, I bided my time and pounced at the first opportunity. It was interesting that these magazines were there in the first place; after all, this was the late sixties and they were definitely banned, considered obscene literature. Moreover, it seemed incongruent in our family, which exuded an energy of repressed sexuality, to entertain this top-shelf smut. But then again, incongruence was the benchmark of all our family conduct.

Initially terrified at being caught, I 'borrowed' one and crept back to my bedroom, excited and encouraged by my brazenness, which proved to be a dictate of future sexual transactions. I had taken a *Playboy*, and as I paged through Hefner's quintessential men's magazine, though the images were tame, even quaint, by today's standards, I was transfixed. Page after page revealed women in various states of near nudity accompanied by inane and banal text in an effort to portray clean and wholesome as opposed to scandalous and pornographic. In spite of, or perhaps because of, old cool-cat Hef's ideal of 'the girl next door with her clothes off', these images succeeded in projecting wanton and lewd sexuality. This dichotomy must have triggered the wayward sexual wiring in my brain because I started to feel aroused and caught up in this sexualisation. I masturbated silently but urgently. Feeling numb and exhausted I crept back into my mother's bedroom to replace the hijacked material.

Notwithstanding my obvious enjoyment at this occurrence, and subscribing to the generally accepted belief that men would react to female sexiness and girls wouldn't, I was puzzled by my behaviour. What did this mean and what did it say about me? Any answers remained unavailable to me and despite feeling very ashamed, I felt compelled to continue my illicit activities, going to extraordinary and sometimes risky lengths to get my little paws on the X-rated mags. I must say that my masturbation, which soon became chronic, was definitely not a healthy expression of my young, curious sexuality – because of the obsessive aspect. What I didn't know then is that when the body is hyper-aroused, it releases neurotransmitters to tranquilise itself. I was thus inducing a self-hypnotic state every time I acted out. It was the perfect complement to my other addictions. I alternated between the different girlie magazines available and at times felt like I was drowning in these stylised effigies of sexual excess. Looking back, I can understand why *Playboy* was my all-time favourite. Some of the models might well have been over eighteen, but all of them were deliberately presented in a grotesque, desperate way to appear as young as possible, with their fresh, innocent faces and pigtails tied with pretty ribbons. I suppose I could identify with them.

My behaviour continued, accompanied by huge self-judgement and condemnation, which served only to reinforce the obsessive patterns. And when the magazines with their clichéd images began to lose their appeal, I found alternative inspiration in the world of romance novels.

I loved reading. It was a world into which I could immerse myself, and since the age of five I had been devouring as many books as I could get access to. A solitary child much of the time, I spent hours closeted in my room and was idyllically happy when engrossed in whatever adventure or detective fiction was my current favourite.

My mother, a keen bibliophile herself, was only too happy to support this diversion, as amongst its obvious benefits was the fact that it was a splendid way to keep me quiet! To be fair, my mother did encourage my love of books, and aside from buying me publications, she took me to the library once or twice a week where I was allowed to make my own 'literary' choices. My bookwormish self strengthened over my teenage years and I waded through some serious books. I also had an Achilles heel for the penny dreadfuls of the day, which translated into Mills & Boon, who published at least ten books a month by various and sundry authors, as well as Barbara Cartland, who mesmerised me with her period pieces of pink prose about romance in an aristocratic culture and, of course, the Angelique books, epic journeys set in seventeenth-century France.

Emboldened by the newly permissive society, writers started pushing their sexual boundaries and hitherto unmentionable topics began to be alluded to in an idealised manner, becoming more graphic all the time. Unconsciously cross-wired to have my sexual energy stimulated by the depictions of sexual abuse in these books, I was at once drawn in and repelled. I felt bad but was unable to examine my attraction; it was too painful. So I acted out my dirty little secret grimly and monotonously; ashamed, yet hooked on its ability to keep me in a sexual trance of nothingness.

I kept all this compartmentalised to stop me from having to face myself, and this resulted in me becoming disconnected not only from myself but also from others. I was terrified that everyone could see how 'corrupt' I was, and so I exhibited a false persona who appeared mostly fine and never needed to ask for help. For years I was caught in this mood altering cycle of arousal and pleasure accompanied by guilt and revulsion. I dare say it was my primary coping mechanism and a major way of getting my needs met without having to pay a cent. It also gave me a sense of control.

Around the time I reached puberty this newfound habit began to lose its appeal as I discovered the real thing; sex. It was inevitable that I would replace the one with the other, acting out the fantasies I'd come across in the magazines and books I'd read. This was the pattern of my life – chasing one high after the next, replacing one obsession with another; the nature of addiction, I suppose.

# 3

## The opposite sex

At twelve, I had never been to a mixed party before. I'd been to girls' parties, sleepovers even, but these had never included boys. The girls at Redhill had been much more interested in riding horses than getting to know the opposite sex.

One of the first mixed parties I went to was that of my cousin, Mark. It was his bar mitzvah celebration and he was having a disco to mark the event. Cousin Mark's claim to family fame was that he had recently lost the sight in one of his eyes due to some dreadful virus, and now sported an eye patch, much like Moshe Dayan, my demigod from the recent Six Day War in Israel. Unlike his heroic look-alike, however, that night Mark was to become a symbol of dishonour (albeit only through my lens).

I can still picture what I looked like that evening. I was wearing a lime-green tent dress – tent dresses being all the rage at the time – with beige trimming around the sleeves and hem. Gold dolly shoes added the finishing touch to the ensemble. My long brown hair was styled like a pineapple, courtesy of Monsieur Habib, the hairdresser of choice for all the northern-suburbs princesses. I was not allowed to wear make-up but, naturally, I had acquired my own private stash which consisted of lipgloss, eyeshadow and mascara. These I would hastily apply in the nearest loo after being dropped off by my parents. I always hoped that the make-up would transform me from Ugly Duckling into Glorious Swan. The truth was that I had a very pretty face, but being overweight seemed to eclipse all this, to my mind. And that night, as I swam in the tent dress, which came down to my dimpled knees, I felt sure that I looked like a house.

I can't recall much of the party itself, except for the incident which resulted in Cousin Mark's aforementioned dishonour. It all began quite innocently with Cousin Mark asking me to dance. I was quite surprised – not that he'd asked me, but because one of the slow songs was playing. We started to shuffle around the floor when the next thing, his hand was on my breast. I was completely mortified and, worse, unable to do anything about it. I wanted to scream, 'Take your hand away, you filthy pig!' But despite how upset I was I did nothing and carried on dancing as if all was well in my world. I am not sure if he made jokes about me then and there to his mates. Maybe he wanted to be seen as a young Lothario. All I know is that I felt bad, shameful and dirty. Like it was my fault and I had done something wrong.

Saddened and confused by the experience, and honouring our family tradition of secrecy, I told no one about what had happened. The shame was stultifying and, if anything, reinforced and strengthened my belief that it was okay for people to treat me however they pleased.

At my new school, the people I made friends with were already accomplished party animals and I soon pushed the memory of that incident to the back of my mind. As I approached my seventeenth birthday I became determined to divest myself of my virgin status. Even with my limited insight I knew that my choice of candidate was no coincidence. He was the son of an old friend of my father. One didn't need to be in Freudian analysis to make an association, and in moments of mad lucidity, drug induced, no doubt, I would joke about how I was looking for my father in the boys I chose.

Conveniently, Prettyboy was escorting me to my matric dance, which gave me a reason to be out till all hours. I was quite calculating. I knew that this would be the night I'd lose my virginity. Far from seeing it as a glorious rite of passage, though, I viewed the impending act as a mere formality, just something I had to get through.

After the dance, as anticipated, he invited me back to his house where, after some token conversation, we found ourselves in his bedroom, minus our clothes. Ever awkward about and uncomfortable in my body, I was grateful for the awful-tasting liquor I had chucked back before leaving my house. Yet despite my inebriation I was still too nervous to participate much in the act – not that he seemed to mind. Instead, I felt myself floating away and above the entire scene, marvelling at how undignified it all was – the sweating and writhing and the animal-like grunts. It was all over quite quickly, and I rolled away from the sticky mess, relieved. I briefly wondered why there hadn't been any blood, but unable to come up with any satisfactory answer, I pushed the thought aside.

I couldn't understand what all the fuss was about. If this was sex, well ... I remember thinking, as our erstwhile and psychopathic minister of police Jimmy Kruger would say callously some five years later in his infamous line, 'It leaves me cold.' Yet when Prettyboy asked the inevitable question, 'So how was it for you?' I answered in an appropriately husky voice, 'It was amazing.' I could feel him glow at my confirmation of his sexual prowess, and that set the stage for future play-acting with men who would be similarly easy to fool.

By my matric year, Hillbrow had become a regular hangout. For any self-respecting drug addict (an oxymoron of note), it was the place to be. Besides being a Mecca for the hippies of the day, it was fabulously cosmopolitan with its mix of nationalities and numerous coffee shops à la Europe. I loved the atmosphere and felt alive and accepted in this parallel universe. Sipping endless cups of coffee at Café Vien, I felt deliciously sophisticated, especially when surrounded by earnest and gorgeous men playing chess and backgammon.

My virginity out of the way, I proceeded to indulge in a number of trysts with dark and dangerous men (for some reason I was always attracted to Europeans), and many furtive fumblings took place in the back of movie houses. Of course I was always out of it. Shortly after the Prettyboy incident I had a short-lived fling with the son of the Persian ambassador – this was while Reza Shah Pahlavi was still on the Persian throne. And then I became completely infatuated with Tommy the Greek, with whom I carried on a torrid affair, secretly, for quite some time. Part of the appeal of these romances lay in their clandestine nature and, being a child of my family, I was an expert in subterfuge. The guys I was with had no idea that my family was completely unaware of this part of my life and, as a result, I could never give out my telephone number or take things to the next level. I also lied about my age. The only time this deception really bothered me was with my Persian prince. I liked him a lot, but by the time I realised this, it was too late to take back all my lies.

The fact that I feared men and occasionally viewed them with contempt was another truth which I kept strictly under wraps, seeing as I was completely dependent on their approval and affirmation. The actual act of sex I found quite distasteful; what turned me on was being desired, and my worth and self-esteem became defined by my sexuality.

After that initial encounter I found myself unable to decline sexual advances. I would want to say no but then a part of me felt obligated to be sexual, as though I had no say over my sexual boundaries. The reality was that I had no boundaries, sexual or otherwise. The sex itself might have left me feeling lonely and empty but, like the masturbation before, it allowed me entry into a trance state, which was an extremely addictive space for me. It became another focus of my attention, a way to hypnotise myself which completely took over my consciousness. This was very powerful stuff. And dangerous.

# 4

## Loss of innocence

After matric I went on holiday to Israel, where I stayed with my great-aunt and -uncle in Tel Aviv. Aunt Rachel was not only a judge but also the first female judge in Israel, to give you an idea of her character. She was hardcore! On my arrival in Israel she went to considerable lengths to warn me about Tel Aviv's 'criminal and lowlife element', which landed up in her court on a regular basis. Of course I paid no attention to her advice, and within days of arriving I met and hooked up with one such lowlife; Goel.

Goel was in his thirties and was handsome in a saturnine kind of way. He was also a big-time drug dealer. (And user, it later transpired.) Like attracting like, Goel spotted me one day at one of Dizengoff Street's more colourful coffee shops and became immediately, and somewhat dangerously, convinced that we were in a relationship. Starved for attention and flattered by his possessiveness, my undeveloped antennae didn't detect the warning signals. As terminally cool as I liked to believe I was, I had yet to develop street smarts.

I would accompany Goel as he walked up Dizengoff Street and down Ben Yehuda, greeting at least half the planet and shaking their hands vigorously. At first, I was impressed by how well connected he was. That is until I realised that what resembled amazing bonhomie was in fact a method of trafficking drug wares. The sheer effrontery and chutzpah he displayed on what was then the Champs-Elysées of Tel Aviv was quite breathtaking. Far from putting me off him, I found his nonchalant criminality exhilarating, even imagining that his reputation rubbed off on me favourably.

Yet somehow, in the midst of this feverish fandango, I began to feel the need to move on. The universe clearly supported this rare moment of rationality, and Yossi entered my space. He was a gorgeous, vibrant Sabra who made me feel beautiful and happy to be alive.

But I had underestimated the persistence of my ex-suitor. After several days of being harassed and of playing hide and seek with a ghostly stalker, I agreed to meet Goel for coffee one late afternoon, whereupon I found myself launching into apologetic explanations, 'I'm so sorry, but I didn't come to Israel to get involved,' I stuttered and stumbled over the words as I tried to put him off gently.

Inscrutable but very calm, he responded, 'I understand, really. But please, won't you come for dinner to meet my parents? I have told them so much about you.' Lulled by his courteousness, my old pattern of being unable to say no was triggered and, disregarding any instinctual wariness on my part, I agreed to be his guest of honour.

We arrived at his place and as I stepped out the car I was taken aback by my surroundings. Through my privileged Johannesburg northern suburb lens, this neighbourhood looked more like a township. Not that I had ever actually set foot in a township, but this was as I imagined one to be – bleak and decrepit. There were no trees, very little colour, and there was sand everywhere. I could hear police vans screeching throughout the neighbourhood. I would later discover that we were in Hatikvah, south of Tel Aviv, and considered to be a symbol of poverty and disadvantage. Vaguely appalled that there were Jewish people living like this, I reflected on my ignorance and snobbishness as I followed him through a narrow alley into a dilapidated low-rise apartment block.

He directed me into a tiny flat up some grimy stairs, and I found myself gushing 'This is lovely' in an effort to compensate for all the less than flattering thoughts that were racing through my head. The walls of the apartment were dirty and peeling, the murky brown carpet worn right through to the cement floor beneath it in places, and there was mould on the ceilings. I noticed there were no curtains in the windows. We entered a room which was empty except for an expensive leather couch, still in its plastic covering. It looked as out of place as I felt. Goel said nothing and suddenly it struck me. This couldn't possibly be his parents' home. In fact it didn't appear to be inhabited by anyone. But even then, when the alarm bells should have been loud enough to alert the National Guard, I remained optimistic.

'So is your family meeting us here?' I asked hopefully.

Goel leant against the doorway of the kitchen, sucking on one of those ghastly Israeli Time cigarettes.

No response. He stared at me, expressionless, and flicked his ash onto the floor.

By this time it was early evening, yet there were no lights on either inside the apartment or outside in the street. The quiet and the darkness were unsettling. I reached for my cigarettes and was about to light one when I noticed a change in Goel. He lost his James Dean pose and sullenness and began walking towards me, a threatening swagger in his movement. It was only when he was standing a step away from me that I noticed the glint in his left hand. To my horror, I saw that he was holding a knife. Eyes boring into mine, he informed me in his somewhat broken English, which up until then had sounded so sexy, that if he couldn't have me, nobody would. Under any other circumstances, those words would have reduced me to hysterical giggles, but looking at his face I did not feel remotely amused, and I started to cry, silently, fat tears coursing down my cheeks as I cursed myself for being so stupid.

Unmoved by my emotion, he took another step forward and grabbed me from behind with his right arm, holding the knife to my throat. His voice was silky and terrifying in my ear.

'My darling, let me tell you what I am going to do to you.'

He ran the knife lightly across my jugular, the pressure just enough to scratch my skin.

He continued in the same hypnotic tone.

'First, I am going to cut you open with this knife,' he purred.

At that point I blanked out mentally, so petrified I could scarcely comprehend the rest of his words as he lovingly described his murderous plans for me. To this day, I believe that my ability to dissociate saved me as I offered no resistance, offering myself up as a willing sacrifice. Perhaps unconsciously I knew that my submission could disarm and neutralise his aggression. I will never know, but after what felt like an eternity, without warning he dropped the knife, opened the front door and pushed me out. Tumbling down the rickety stairs, I fell out onto the deserted street outside.

I have no idea how long I wandered around in the darkness, disoriented and in shock, before a fairy godfather in the form of a taxi driver stopped to see if I needed assistance. I began to shake uncontrollably as the reality of what had happened, the danger I had been in, hit me, but thankfully my rescuer asked no questions and transported me right to the door of my aunt's apartment.

By then it was after twelve. I slunk into the flat, by this time recomposed, calm, even. In fact I was starting to doubt my own reality, a rather insidious but all too familiar pattern. As I tiptoed to my bedroom I fell over my aunt who, worried, was waiting up for me. A part of me wished I could fling myself into her arms and cry it all away, but I didn't have the faintest idea how to do something like that. So, banishing that childish thought, I offered up a sanitised version of what had happened, fearful that she might want to send me home.

In fairness, and with the paucity of what I related, she tried to understand and to help, but I believe that it was really difficult to support me then. At the time I was so rebellious and defiant – an attitude made tangible by the cross I wore in my right ear. The cross did not represent any Christian crusade on my part; it was more to engender shock, something at which I excelled. And it certainly pushed the buttons of my conservative family in Israel. I am sure I offended them and I guess I could have been more circumspect around this issue. For years to come, my uncle in Hadera would refer to 'that girl with the tsalem (cross) in her ear'.

Assuring my aunt of my okayness – as if I would allow a 'lowlife' like that to get to me – I dragged myself to my room and for the next few days once again relied on the adaptive nature of the mind to shut down the incident so that I neither registered nor felt the pain. But it did leave me in an obviously fragile space.

It was at this point that my real exploration of Israel began, and for this I have my great-aunt and -uncle to thank, particularly my uncle Avraham. I am convinced that the outcome of Israel would have been very different without him to temper my unrestrained chaos.

My great-uncle was a celebrated general in the Israeli Army and at the age of twenty-eight had been commanding officer of all Haganah personnel in the Jewish Brigade. In the War of Independence in 1948 he was put in charge of the 7th brigade. He was also the kindest man I had ever met and a natural-born storyteller. He would expound on numerous and diverse topics and really took an interest in me – the person behind my various defenses. Although I was not able to confide in him about Goel, his unconditional acceptance was balm to my troubled soul and I remain grateful to him for this.

When I'd first arrived in Tel Aviv, my aunt and uncle had left me to my own devices. Clearly I had not been able to handle this unfettered freedom and now my aunt took over. Forcing me to start behaving like a tourist and sightseer, she promptly packed me off on an organised trip through Israel. I particularly loved the old city in Jerusalem, which took me to the Western Wall or Wailing Wall, as it is better known due to the nature of the prayers said there. It is believed that divine presence continues to reside there, so praying there is like praying directly to God through the wall. As I offered my prayer written on paper, which I then slipped through a crack in the wall, I became uncharacteristically emotional as I thought of all the people who had stood there before me. In that moment I felt proud to be a Jewess.

I also enjoyed the Arab marketplace which was bursting with colours and exotic smells. I learnt to haggle prices and bought an exquisite Ethiopian silver necklace which I kept for many years. At each new vendor I would drink small cups of very strong coffee as it was considered impolite to refuse.

We arrived in Bethlehem on Christmas Day and I couldn't help feeling a bit overwhelmed by all the celebrations going on. However, what I remember most clearly about Bethlehem was the beautiful Bedouin-type dress I bought at the marketplace there. It was black with sparkling chips of mirrors all over the front.

Next we went to Masada, which then was synonymous with courage and freedom. Perhaps the climate is different today but then my spirit resonated with its history of mystery and political intrigue. My hero, Moshe Dayan, had initiated the practice of holding the swearing-in ceremony for soldiers who had completed their basic training on top of Masada. The ceremony ended with the declaration, 'Masada shall not fall again.' As I stood on this site of ancient palaces, I felt connected to its rugged beauty. In fact, I felt impossibly alive, in a way I have rarely if ever felt since.

This tour and especially my experience in Masada was enough to sustain and contain me for my remaining weeks in the Holy Land, and as I sat on the plane flying home I felt bittersweet about leaving.

On returning, my memories of that holiday faded into a film noir, complete with sepia tones and unresolved conclusion. Not even my good experiences were allowed the luxury of colour. When friends and family quizzed, 'So how was your trip?' I would glibly answer, 'I have a love/hate relationship with Israel.' This inane but enigmatic response had the effect of silencing all further conversation.

About six months later, I fell into a disabling depression. My experiences were intruding into my consciousness and I didn't know how to deal with them. Then one night, really struggling with my jagged mood, my desperation and longing to be understood overcame any good sense and I went through to my mother and Johnnie's bedroom, whereupon I compulsively disclosed to them what had happened in Israel.

My admission, which, I suppose, was my way of asking for help, was met by thinly disguised disbelief. Devastated, I could only assume that my aunt had communicated her displeasure at my attitude and concern about my behaviour to my mother, which had affected their opinion of me. I would never know. I felt humiliated and abandoned by their judgement and suspicion and vowed never again to entrust them with my feelings.

Notwithstanding this resolve, a few months later I found myself once again trying to win my father's approval when I went to visit him in London.

# 5

# Fall from grace

By the time I was twenty, the weight that had enveloped me like a shroud for most of my life, ill fitting but at the same time comfortable in its disguise, had fallen away, revealing a beautiful, svelte me. For a brief period, I was delighted at this metamorphosis. Suddenly I was the sought-after flavour of the moment. Jewish boys, who previously wouldn't have looked at me once, let alone twice, were calling to ask me out. I found the affirmation too hard to resist and, for a time, became quite frivolous.

I dazzled myself with a string of good-looking studs to convince me of my newfound desirability. While in Port Elizabeth visiting my cousin, I hunted down two friends of my father from days gone by and seduced both of them. Next, I embarked on two successive cloak and dagger affairs with the boyfriends of very good friends of mine. I was immune to whom I hurt, caring only about myself. Yet I wasn't happy, and I couldn't understand why. Wasn't this what I'd been yearning for all my life? Acceptance and admiration?

I decided the answer to happiness lay in losing more weight. So I stopped eating, and fell in love with my jutting hipbones, touching them constantly just to check that they hadn't disappeared in the last five minutes. The thinner I became, the prettier I felt, and the mounting concern of family and friends only served to spur me on.

I despised myself for having to eat at all, and felt shame for experiencing hunger. Actually it was not so much hunger I experienced as starvation. But I was so out of touch with my body that I was incapable of identifying sensations of hunger or even thirst, and remained in this state of semi-starvation for years, my obsession to be thin injuring and overruling my survival instincts.

Around the time I embarked on my slow and torturous journey of self-deprivation I started, reluctantly, to undergo a very lengthy dental procedure. Evidently most of my teeth needed crowning (probably from all the sweets I'd consumed over the years), and before that could be achieved, root treatment needed to be done.

This turned out to be a long and laborious process during which whatever could go wrong did (bearing in mind that this was over thirty years ago when technology was not what it is today). As time went by, I started to feel like Dustin Hoffman in *The Marathon Man* and my endodontist not unlike his evil protagonist Dr Christian Szell (who was based on the Angel of Death himself, Dr Josef Mengele). Suffice it to say, he was not possessed of the kindest dental chair-side manners. Unmoved by my suffering, he didn't bother to hide his increasing irritation at my low pain threshold – probably affected by years of using cough mixtures, which had increased my tolerance for the seemingly endless amount of injections he gave me before he could even touch my mouth. I am sure he thought I was being deliberately oppositional and weak in my unwillingness to withstand a bit of pain, as his oft-repeated line was, 'This really won't hurt.'

Paradoxically, having remained silent for years, my mouth now refused to be numbed despite enough anaesthetic to dull an elephant. I was reduced to a quivering wreck by this violent and ongoing assault on my mouth until finally, when the pain was simply unendurable, 'Dr Szell' gave me Stopayne tablets. At the time I felt that without them I would have lost my mind. The irony was that I lost it anyway, as I soon became addicted to the stuff.

From the time I took the first lime green pill of sublimity – or rather mediocrity – Stopayne and I would not be parted except during my pregnancy and the few times that I unavoidably ran out, usually when I was overseas.

I had a strange habit then of attributing gender to the various drugs I took. For instance, Phensydyl was decidedly male in its ability to stomp all over me, and Valoron, which came later, I saw as being female with its subtler, soothing qualities. Yet curiously, and despite its unbelievable hold over me, Stopayne was genderless. Even with its particular qualities, such as the addition of meprobamate (a highly addictive sedative) to its more classical cocktail of codeine, caffeine and paracetamol, it remained somehow generic in my mind.

In October of 1976, as my twenty-first birthday loomed, I started to make arrangements to travel overseas. My father, Mervyn, had invited me to stay with him and his wife Sophie in their London apartment. At some point during that past year, my entire family had become more civilised, at least outwardly, and had begun talking to one another. In a way this made life easier, yet it was also unsettling, as I knew it was almost entirely an act and that simmering close to the surface there was always the threat of true feelings exposing this happy family for what it really was.

It was during this time of supposed conviviality that the invitation to visit my father was extended to me. Though I pretended to be completely blasé about its meaning and feigned indifference, particularly in front of my mother who, I believed, still carried a very bright and sad torch for him, secretly I was thrilled, though nervous. After all the years of his passive indifference and rejection, I believed my father might finally be prepared to accept and love me. After all, I was thin now. Wouldn't that make everything fabulous?

I continued my cycle of not eating and revelled in my newfound feelings of sexiness. I ate the absolute bare minimum necessary to allay suspicions and hugged my precious eating disorder close to my heart and protruding ribs. I might not have been eating, but my obsession around food raged on in my head incessantly. I also developed body image disorder. I would look in the mirror and be reasonably okay with what I saw. Then five minutes later I would look again and see the Michelin woman reflected back to me and be completely thrown by the experience. I knew, intellectually, that it was impossible to have gained ten kilos in five minutes, but my feelings were so powerful and convincing that it was hard to discount them.

Exhausted though I was by my strict eating regime, my twenty-first birthday party went off well. My mother really came through for me and pretty much gave me carte blanche. I decided on Arabian Nights as the theme, and our gardens, which to me had always felt enchanted, provided the perfect setting. La Concorde, a restaurant in town, was chosen to do the catering; lamb on a spit and an appropriate Middle Eastern menu 'fit for a king', or in this case, a queen, was promised. My colour scheme was purple, from the invitations to the purple and cream marquee that arrived days before the party. We (my mother, sister and I) now had the structure and in order to create the right ambience we hired and in some cases bought cushions in every size and description, conjuring a harem-type atmosphere. It was quite spectacular.

On the night, everyone entered fully into the spirit of the theme. Sid, Ca's husband, was blue-blooded as always and came dressed as a Turkish prince, while Ca was strikingly outfitted in turquoise harem pants and a cropped top with sequins all over. They looked delightful. Everyone in my family participated and even Mom and Johnnie dressed up. But it was my baby brother Phil who stole the show, and I daresay some hearts, by appearing as a young Persian prince wearing white pants with a red cummerbund and a white turban. That get-up, combined with his white-blond hair, made him a photographer's dream. And as for myself, I had hired the most gorgeous dress. Black with silver sequins, it hugged every inch of my body yet fell gracefully where it needed to. I had never worn anything like it before. I felt sultrily sexy and, looking back, if I say so myself, I was quite the showstopper! At the time, the piece de resistance for me was not my appearance but who I had on my arm, and I was thrilled to the core to have Supermodel as my date. We had met a few weeks previously and he had agreed to accompany me to my party. An attorney in training, he was also the most beautiful man I had ever met. When he arrived wearing a deep navy kimono type jacket which revealed his bronzed torso, I nearly swooned! My friends were blown away by me and him, and so my night was made. It tarnished only somewhat when Supermodel suggested, 'Come Jo, let's go and make love at my place.' As always I felt unable to say no, and although I didn't really want to leave my own party, my need to please was too strong. I certainly didn't enjoy how I felt after half an hour of purple passion, but I managed to wave it away with my general excitement at being twenty-one. The day after the party, I began counting down the sleeps till my departure. A slight damper on my enthusiasm was the unfortunate coincidence of a dental appointment scheduled on the morning of the big day. All seemed to be going well until on my way out, as an afterthought, Dr Szell remarked quite cavalierly, 'Oh, by the way, there is a small chance that your tooth could react to the flight. But I'm sure you'll be fine!'

I'm sure you'll be fine? I shuddered to think what that could mean, Dr Szell's idea of pain being so vastly different from mine. Nothing about this so-called recreation of my mouth had been smooth and pain-free so far. Why would this be any different?

So I set off in trepidation, preparing to wing my way across the skies with my tooth like an explosive device set to be triggered by a change in altitude. I felt as if I were inhabited by a suicide bomber about to wreak havoc on my being. It was too late to cancel my flight, though, and besides, nobody would have understood. They'd just have thought I was being melodramatic.

I boarded my flight and prepared myself for the inevitable. Back then one could still smoke, so I immediately lit up and proceeded to puff away nervously, which no doubt didn't help things. When I had made my way through half a pack of John Player Specials without any 'reactions', I began to wonder if perhaps I'd been lucky. But then it happened. It was as if my tooth had detonated and imploded inwards and down towards the bottom of my face. The rest of the journey was hell. My mouth had become infected, and although there was a doctor on board, his medication was no rival for my own, and completely ineffectual.

It was in this state that I arrived at Heathrow for my reunion with my father. Swollen-faced, tearful and with an excruciating headache, I located him.

'My mouth is infected,' I told him, slurring through swollen lips. 'I need to find a dentist. It hurts!' I broke down in sobs.

He seemed quite taken aback by my desperation, and unsure how to react. Frowning, he answered, 'Let's go home and I'll think about what to do.'

Distressed by his abrupt response on the one hand, but too sore to care on the other, I meekly followed him out, both of us sucking on cigarettes.

We arrived at his place, the penthouse on the top floor of a 42-storey skyscraper in the middle of the city; the new and not quite finished Barbican Complex. It was hugely imposing, and despite its opulence and the fact that it was apparently architecturally significant, I found its contemporary aesthetics quite dark and grim. I was impressed by the fact that we were met by a doorman, though.

Inside the penthouse there were massive windows with amazing views over London. The decor was modern; in the lounge there was a shaggy white rug on the floor and a coffee table made of glass and steel. Sophie was sitting on one of the large black leather couches in the centre of the room. This was the first time I had met her in person, and I had not been prepared for how gorgeous she was. She reminded me of the model Jean Shrimpton, minus the fringe. Tall, with shoulder-length brown hair, she was dressed in jeans and a short, close-fitting top which showed off her slender figure. She had a beautiful face – big brown eyes, high cheekbones, a retroussé nose and perfect, cherry-coloured lips. She was not a lot older than me and, like me, initially eager to please.

'Hi Jo!' She spoke in a surprisingly plummy accent, considering that she hailed from Pretoria. 'Let me show you your room.' She took my arm and escorted me to the guest room at the back of the apartment. It was simply but elegantly furnished and I was happy to see that it had an en suite bathroom.

Once Mervyn had gathered himself, he did his best to help me (which translated into delegating to Sophie), and the next few days whirled by in a haze of dentists, antibiotics and painkillers, after which my terrorist tooth settled down. Mervyn was full of compliments for the new and clearly improved version of myself, and paraded me around his local pubs, showing me off to all his cronies. He visibly preened when one of his mates leeringly remarked, 'Wow Merv, you are one lucky bastard to have two such beautiful girls.' Banal words indeed, but I was actually flattered, craving attention as I did, and even though the compliment was directed more at Mervyn.

As much as I needed everything to be perfect, I was becoming conscious of my father and Sophie's drinking patterns, which seemed to be worryingly habitual. And even though I was starting to enjoy the heavy-handed Bloody Marys that Mervyn frequently dispensed, I couldn't help feeling uneasy about the amount of alcohol that was flowing so freely. Early one Sunday morning I bumped into him in the kitchen where he was opening a beer that he had taken from the fridge. He must have seen the expression on my face because he explained, 'I've been having problems with my stomach, so I can't drink coffee or tea anymore.'

'Oh, yes, of course,' I replied, as if that were a perfectly normal, adequate explanation for why one would be drinking beer at 8 am on a Sunday morning. I registered the incongruence somewhere within me, but my capacity for denial was such that I would only realise the extent of his alcoholism years later.

As the days went by, Mervyn's behaviour became decidedly bizarre. His conversations with me grew increasingly unsettling as he asked more and more questions, some of them quite personal and sexual in nature. But uncomfortable as these questions made me feel, it seemed churlish to refuse to satisfy what appeared to be genuine interest. Understandably, I thought, he had not seen me in years and would want to catch up and get to know his long-lost daughter. What I was not able to acknowledge or recognise then was the atmosphere of cloying seduction pervading that flat, created and encouraged by my father, and my own sense of violation because of it.

It was hard to put a finger on exactly what created this atmosphere. In some ways, the situation was perfectly benign. Each day followed a similar routine; in the morning we would have coffee and breakfast together at the glass dining room table and then I would spend most of the day exploring London – its shops in particular. Sophie was quite shocked at my shopping habits – as the pound was more favourable in terms of the rand than it had ever been, I was determined to take advantage of this and was shopping up a storm. Horrified, she would reproach me in a high-pitched voice at each purchase, 'Joanne, you cannot spend that amount on a pair of boots!' Well, I could and I did. Besides, it wasn't her money, it was mine (from my twenty-first), which brought up a whole lot of feelings around money and my father – he had never paid a cent of maintenance. But I didn't really feel like going down that road, and fortunately my friend Elly arrived in London and so I had a new shopping partner.

Dinners were usually spent with Sophie and Mervyn at their favourite pub or at a nearby restaurant. Pleasant enough affairs. But, dimly, I was aware of something off in his constant comments about Sophie and other women's appearance, his needling me for information about my past encounters with men, the way he would touch Sophie in my presence, which even though I was technically an adult, in hindsight I can see was not appropriate behaviour, and the thinly disguised sexual innuendos in much of what he said. I didn't want to acknowledge what was happening as then I'd have had to face some uncomfortable truths. But it seemed he was using the two of us to maintain some sort of state of arousal.

At first, desperate to continue to receive his approval, however conditional, I convinced myself it was okay to keep up the pretence that everything was normal and above board. I had started dating someone in Johannesburg, who happened to be in London at the same time as me. Nothing much had happened between us physically and, having ascertained this, Mervyn took it upon himself to orchestrate an evening for the two of us so that Justin could spend the night and we could have sex. When I demurred, Mervyn became petulant and labelled me 'pathologically prudish'. Patronisingly, he informed me, 'I suppose it's because you live in South Africa that you can't help being provincial and narrow-minded. It's not your fault.'

Duty bound, he condescended to 'educate' me and, the very next night I found myself being escorted to the Raymond Revue Bar. As we made our way towards the theatre building, still unsure of what to expect, bright, traffic-red lights in oversized letters proclaimed 'World Centre of Erotic Entertainment'. Not having had a red-letter day up until that point, perhaps it signified a night to remember? Certainly the evening would be memorable, but in ways that I would sooner forget than celebrate.

Inside, I found I was the only female amongst at least fifty men, made up of a more or less equal mix of Japanese businessmen knocking back their drinks like water, and the darlings of the moment, an array of Middle Eastern oil sheiks or wannabes who were currently haemorrhaging their petrodollars all around London. Clearly their prodigious talent for spending included the night life in Soho.

Mervyn handed me some vile-tasting cocktail; but at least it was liquor, which I gratefully sipped, and as I sat back on a plush velvet chair I ruminated about Mervyn's need to make me part of his world. As unevolved as I was, I knew that I was there as an accessory to his addiction. My father assured me that the show was 'very tasteful' and 'artistic', which nearly made me choke on the noxious concoction that I was drinking. The show started and every now and again Mervyn would lean toward me conspiratorially and say something like 'Doesn't that girl have great tits?' Unwilling as I was to participate in this fantasy of his, I lacked the boundaries to refuse to take part, or to get up and leave. So I sat there, willing myself into a semi-dissociative space in order to cope with what was happening around me.

The Raymond Revue Bar might still have had delusions of grandeur based on its past glories, but by then it was nothing more than a nudie show masquerading as art, and about as exciting as a used condom. Eventually, after the dramatic concluding act, or climax, it was time to leave, and as we made our way home in the taxi, Mervyn talked excitedly about the 'girls' we had seen, clearly expecting me to share in his enthusiasm. But as I listened to his words I thought about the position of women in a world where we were referred to as 'girls' or 'ladies', never women, a culture in which men in particular needed to infantilise women to make themselves feel in control. And my own father was at the centre of all this. It was at this point that my image of him shattered. As much as I continued to want Mervyn's affirmation, I no longer felt unquestioning admiration for him, and after that night, I stopped placing him on a pedestal.

At the same time, and I don't believe coincidentally, the first real evidence of my bipolar mood disorder emerged – I began to behave quite erratically, spending more than ever, talking louder and faster, and sleeping around. It was then that I gave a name to my as yet-undiagnosed disease; Ladymania. It's strange that I chose to personify it as a lady, not a woman, but if I think about it now, for me there is a difference between the two terms, 'lady' being somewhat less serious than 'woman'. Which makes sense in that for a long time I denied the seriousness of my illness. Although during Ladymania's first visit my mood did not elevate to the dangerous levels that I would encounter in later years, it was high enough to give me the energy and courage I needed to leave the Brodie's gilded cage of ambiguity, and with the help of my mother and Johnnie, who happened to be in London at the same time, I booked myself into a bed and breakfast in Knightsbridge for the remaining ten days of my stay.

Euphoric, I engaged in a ritual dance of war and gleefully celebrated my 'escape' by spending fortunes of money on instant gratification. Prestigious and acclaimed designer label boutiques were non-existent in South Africa, and the sweetening powers of overdosing on Gucci were not to be underestimated. Frenzied and feverish, I shopped myself into oblivion and was enraptured by every moment. I also performed my rather scandalous version of Salomé in the Dance of the Seven Veils as I embarked on a binge of sexual excess which included one of my taxi drivers, an Egyptian who stayed in the same block (my creative contribution in promoting Jewish–Egyptian détente, I thought wickedly), and the son of a friend of my stepfather.

I wish I could say that I was headed for the path of deeper spirituality, looking for ways to shed my 'veils' of illusions, but regrettably the only journey that I was on was that of increasingly violent self-destruction.

# 6

# Looking for a way out

By the time I left London, my relationship with my father had sunk into an abyss of resentment and disowned feelings, and I flew home without saying goodbye. Coming from a family in which certain aunts and uncles hadn't spoken to one another for decades, the art of emotional cut-offs was in my blood.

Back in Johannesburg, I was ill at ease and restless. I struggled to settle down to my life, unsure what to do next. I was dimly aware of having experienced some ordeal, but far from having come through it a stronger or wiser person, it felt like I was suffering an aftermath of sorts.

I tried to sound sophisticated when recounting my 'risqué adventures' in London, in this way normalising the abnormal and preventing myself from having to deal with reality. At the same time, I publicly denounced Mervyn as a bastard whom I 'never wanted to see again', without ever explaining, or perhaps realising, why.

Limited in my responses, I only knew how to blame or to self-blame, or a combination of both. The difficult part was acknowledging what I was blaming for.

I felt directionless, which wasn't necessarily a new situation. Although on one level certain that I had talent, I seemed to sabotage all creative efforts at 'finding myself'; fear of failure and success weighed equally heavy. I secretly yearned for academic glory, but despite two independent BA registrations at Wits University I never completed more than the first year of either, and only ever achieved good grades in French, a subject and language that for some reason flowed for me.

Despite my lack of intellectual forbearance, I was quite a serious person, and in between devouring the latest bestseller fiction, I went through a brief but intense literary phase – my bluestocking period. In a strange and bleak space, I was drawn to writers that mirrored my internal state and waded through works such as Jean Genet's play *The Balcony*. I was intrigued by his obsession with sex and prostitution. The play takes place in a brothel where common men play men of power in their sexual fantasies. It not only exposes the emptiness of societal roles but also shows how fantasy, rather than making reality more palatable, can actually contaminate reality when acted out.

My reading matter of choice was enough to depress the most indomitable spirit, and mine was quite damaged to begin with. Having concluded that life was meaningless, I became determined to understand Jean Paul Sartre. Although I was unable to decipher much of his writing, I nevertheless recognised in it my own cynicism and despair.

I knew for sure that I was in crisis, existential or otherwise, as I started to entertain more and more thoughts of suicide. Once they had arrived, these thoughts refused to leave, and soon took up permanent residence in my head. Far from scaring me, they comforted me with their promise of a way out. Cushioned by my secret strategy, which was as powerful as it was mind altering, my mood lifted. And though I felt better for a time, this in no way prevented the inevitable moment when I found myself in front of my mother's bathroom cabinet, taking out a bottle of Mogadon sleeping tablets and swallowing the entire contents.

A little shocked by my action and unsure of what to do next, I went to lie down and hoped that I would drift away into the eternal arms of Morpheus. Whether I thought I was my own version of Sleeping Beauty and would only sleep for a while will remain forever moot, because the Fates intervened and the telephone rang, piercing my slumberous state. I remember shouting dementedly, 'Fuck, that's loud enough to wake the dead!' (no pun intended) as I lurched to answer it. It was my aunt, 'The Queen', and, really benzoed now, I confessed the overdose in a drunken orgy of self-disclosure.

She called her doctor, who, in his words 'drove over rooftops' to reach me. I was rushed to a clinic where I suffered the first of what would be many stomach washes over the years, and after a precautionary overnight stay, was released the following morning. Initially chastened by my near-death experience and grateful to be alive, this would not be the learning experience I might have expected. In fact the exact opposite was true. This was merely the first in many such attempts I would make on my life.

Family and friends were caring and solicitous, and I thrived on all the attention. I felt loved and supported until I overheard a conversation between The Queen, my mother and stepfather, in which they discussed my 'lack of remorse' and my enjoyment of the tragedy queen role that I had supposedly embraced. Stung by the truth, I felt judged and criticised, and defended myself by withdrawing further and plotting to move out of home. This proved to be a Herculean task, as I was not self-supporting, and 'nice Jewish girls' did not live alone.

As the months went by, I came no closer to my goal of moving out, until one day it dawned on me. The only way to leave home and to avoid conflict was to get married. So I put myself out there and was introduced to Stephen, a handsome, dark-haired man with piercing blue eyes. I liked him and we started dating immediately.

Within eight months we were married, fairytale wedding dress and all. I remember walking down the aisle and feeling saddened by my compliance with other people's realities. What I also didn't know as I walked towards matrimonial bliss was that I was pregnant, which clearly accounted for the recent increase in my cup-size. Somehow this latest development made sense to me, and against the advice of everyone, I made the decision to go ahead with my pregnancy. It wasn't that I felt particularly motherly because, frankly, I didn't have the faintest idea how to be maternal, but I knew instinctively that this was my only chance to have a child; it was now or never.

So for once in my life, I pitched up for the process and managed to give birth to my amazing son, Darren. I loved being pregnant. It was the one time in my life when I didn't care about my weight, and although I thought I looked as huge as the Michelin Man, I felt so healthy. I had even stopped taking my daily cocktail of Obex and Stopayne.

Giving birth was another story. I had this gynae who believed in natural childbirth. Whatever its supposed benefits, they certainly didn't help me as I was in labour for nearly twenty-four hours! I ended up having an epidural at the last minute, and just at the point where he was considering giving me a Caesar, my son was born – the most perfect creature I had ever seen.

My mom organised a nursing sister to help me for a few weeks, and I was hugely grateful as in the beginning I was terrified of doing something wrong – I was even too scared to bath him, just in case I dropped him. In fact, Stephen was the first to give Darren a bath! It took me time to adjust, but then it was all fine. Darren was the most amazing baby. He was so good right from the start, seldom throwing tantrums or fussing over his food.

While having Darren was the best thing that had happened in my life, and I loved his presence, I found the reality and enormity of living with my husband on a day-to-day basis unbearable. And as for the sex … Well, more to the point, the lack thereof; we did not have sex, not if I could help it. I simply could not go through with it and can literally count on my one hand the number of times we had sex in the three and a half years we stayed married. It felt too real, too intrusive, too close, and I was repelled by feelings that I could not push away or repress.

Anonymous sex was easy for me, but so-called intimacy was a struggle that I was not up for at the time. Isolated, with no one to speak to, I felt like a stranger marking time and living a lie. My life carried on in a fog of suburban obscurity as I tried to be a 'good girl'. Still caught up in make-believe, I was playing 'housey-housey' as seen through the lens of my mother. Of course I was bound to meet resistance as Stephen had his own views of the ideal marriage.

The fact is I think that he was ready to settle down while I didn't know what I wanted. I do think that in some areas he was more mature than I was. And as far as the sex issue was concerned he certainly tried. He came to me the one day and said 'Jo, we need to talk, I know you masturbate and …' Well, when he said that I was so overcome with shame that I blocked out the rest of his words and ended the conversation as soon as possible.

Of course, in other areas he could be as stubborn as a mule. For instance he would insist on having one of those La-Z-Boy chairs, which in those days came in either brown or black. I loathed them. To me they represented the height of middle-class mediocrity, but then again, this opinion was heavily influenced by my mother's thinking.

Amidst all our personal drama, we had some fun times too. We went on lovely holidays to the Cape and travelled on the Blue Train. For a while we were good friends, and he was always a fantastic father. But this conviviality could not last, as Stephen became increasingly frustrated with my inability to fulfil what he perceived as my wifely duties. A cold war ensued, reaching the point where we stopped talking. The closest I can come to describing the atmosphere in our relationship is 'wooden', a word which also mirrored the beige and brown scheme predominating our newly built house.

The only space that I was allowed to decorate was the guest loo. Naturally, this was the prettiest room of all, and its beautiful fragrance and elegant colours were at least a reminder of other possibilities.

I thought a lot about leaving and then just when I felt it was all becoming too much, I experienced a pharmaceutical epiphany. I had been walking around for days with a headache worse than Quasimodo's until finally, one nasty lumbar puncture later, I was diagnosed with encephalitis. Considering that I wasn't actively dealing with anything in my life, and was living in my head (not a particularly well place to be), I am not surprised that I manifested an inflammation of the brain.

Metaphysical insight aside, I was put to bed for some weeks to recover. I loved being sick. It was a legitimate way of getting love and support from friends and family, and when the Stopayne did nothing to curb the onslaught happening at the back of my head, my neurologist was more than happy to up the ante and prescribed Valoron, an opioid analgesic similar to morphine. Now those were painkillers; exquisite little red beauties in capsules or drops which would numb me out, take away all the noise in my head and for a while leave me floating in disembodied delight. I was devoted from the start.

As far as my addiction was concerned, those were some of the golden days, as I languished idly viewing, amongst others, my all-time favourite television series *The Professionals* on our recently acquired video machine. And I didn't have to think up stories about why I didn't want to or couldn't have sex. It almost seemed too good to be true. My only concern, which I completely underestimated, was that I would need to make a plan to continue to obtain Valoron once I was better. Being a Schedule 7 medication, it would not be as easy to procure as my other drugs.

However, I was incredibly resourceful, albeit only when it came to my addiction. I extended the sell-by date of my headaches and managed to manipulate scripts from my unsuspecting neurologist, which gave me some breathing space while I looked for a more permanent and satisfactory arrangement.

Somewhat reluctantly, I recovered, and life went back to whatever normal was. I might have carried on sleepwalking my way through domestic monotony had it not been for a particular weekend that would change my life irrevocably.

My friends Kelly and Roland were in town and I had invited them for afternoon tea. When they arrived the first thing I noticed was how amazing they looked. They had always been a great-looking couple, but something had changed – I couldn't quite put my finger on what it was, but they seemed somehow brighter and more vibrant than before. Kelly, who was slim to start off with, had lost some weight, and Roland was looking particularly handsome. Looking at this glowing couple, I wanted what they had. What they had, it transpired, was a large quantity of white powder. This Roland carefully produced from his top pocket an hour or so after they arrived. I was so excited he might as well have been pulling white rabbits out his jacket. I couldn't wait for my turn as I watched him chop lines on the mirror in front of him.

Cocaine was my wild card. From the very first line I remember musing, 'If I could only have this feeling for the rest of my life, all would be well.' My first sniff of blow transported me into a world where I felt clever, confident, beautiful and invincible; everything and more that I had craved my entire life. Before leaving, Roland gave me a couple of grams, and as I stashed them away, I assured myself that I would use only on special occasions. My intentions might have been honourable but I found myself sneaking frequent visits to my secret hiding place. And so I went straight from experimentation to full-on dependence, bypassing all other stages of addiction as I pursued its 'allure of more' with about as much subtlety and moderation as Grace Mugabe in a Ferragamo shoe store. Shortly after beginning my relationship with the Lady in White, I read a comprehensive article in *Time* magazine entitled 'Middle Class High', which seemed to affirm my lifestyle choices and make my using seem respectable. 'After all,' I reasoned, 'I am only chasing the all-American dream, so doesn't that make it mainstream and acceptable?' And even when, further in the article, I read what should have been an ominous warning, it was easy for me to gloss over this part. The interviewee was quoted as saying, 'After one hit of cocaine, I feel like a new man. The only problem is the first thing the new man wants is another hit.' Actually, I was delighted to see my own feelings so expressively articulated by someone else, and in *Time* magazine, nogal!

The next nine months of my life were a constant effort to maintain my manufactured sense of self. It was not only the cocaine but what it represented that changed me. I became dissatisfied with my life and, like my drug, I wanted more of anything and everything. The coke might have become middle class, but it was still synonymous with a first-class image, and I quickly developed delusions of grandeur around being one of a small band of elite cokeheads. Apart from Roland and Kelly there were the equally glamorous Robert and Bella, Pete, who was a journalist, and Kate and Jeannie, a lesbian couple. They were all a bit older than me so I never quite fitted in, but this never stopped me from trying really hard. I went from dowdy and frumpy to New Wave meets New Romantics and discovered that clothes and music were an integral part of the package. There were two shops that I frequented at this time. The one was in Yeoville and catered for the 'alternative lifestyle'. Here I found delightfully provocative clothes, such as bright red pirate-style knickerbockers and lots of skinny ties in gold and silver. The other shop, which was in Rosebank, stocked clothes which I was convinced were especially created for me, and at any one time I had more ruffles and swirls of taffeta, chiffon and georgette than the Elizabethan Queen and all her ladies in waiting. I remember one outfit which consisted of black pants, a gold bodice and a jacket with ruffles on the sleeves and collar, topped off with gold hairspray, which in those days was a rare and much coveted item of beautification. It was a statement of note!

The music was eclectic too; I remember listening to a lot of The

Cars, The Cure and Elvis Costello. My theme song was 'Tainted Love' by Soft Cell, which I adored. But I must admit I was going through a major reggae phase and would play Bob Marley endlessly, as well as artists like Max Romeo and Linton Kwesi Johnson (LKJ), a British-based reggae dub poet. Somewhere during this time, I found my voice and asked for a divorce. It almost became acrimonious, but my need to have a clean break as quickly as possible meant that I settled, despite my lawyers' stern admonishments about 'later regrets'. Darren and I moved out into a lovely apartment in Illovo and so began our new life. I was relieved to find myself newly single in almost unheard of record time. Stephen and I hovered between tensely polite and seriously strained, ultimately settling on civil, which was better for all of us, particularly Darren, who was only three and a half.

The dealer I was using had moved to Swaziland and so I began to spend inordinate amounts of time with him and his wife in the small and pretty kingdom. There was usually an assortment of other camp followers who were all there for the same reason. I have been extremely self-absorbed over the years but those months must go down as the most vainglorious of times. I thought only about how I looked; life was on the outside, never on the inside. The other women and I spent hours in front of the mirror dressing up and liberally applying our cosmetic warpaint before heading off to some or other night-time festivity. One night at about midnight, suitably bedecked and completely trashed, we went off to the Royal Swazi casino. Not to gamble but to be oohed and aahed over. We were living on the borrowed energy of a seemingly endless reservoir of shimmering white flake.

One couldn't be overdressed, and I began to wear resplendent though outlandish outfits in lustrous fabrics as befitted my new flamboyance. I remember a peacock-coloured school-boy jacket with ruffles topped off with a pair of bright flamingo-pink sunglasses. The sunglasses were a complete driving health hazard in that it was impossible to identify red robots through their screaming fuchsia shades, but hey! What's the price of vanity? I also had a T-shirt that screeched 'Enjoy Cocaine' in the same lettering as Coca Cola's slogan of the day. It was a hoot, and I couldn't understand why people were disgusted by it. Some of the more ostentatious members of the cocaine cult advertised their association by wearing chains with tiny silver or gold spoons which signalled their status. At heart an arriviste, I coveted this vulgar item and am sure that I would have found a way to commission one had it not been for a rapid change in my economic circumstances.

La Dama Blanca was proving to be a very demanding mistress and I was struggling to keep up emotionally, financially and physically, as even I could no longer ignore the obvious signs of my obsession. My dealer's wife, who was my equal when it came to using, and I would go supermarket shopping and not even half way through, we would stop, completely exhausted and unable to carry on without a pick-me-up in the form of a cocaine-filled cigarette, which we would smoke in the store, oblivious to our surroundings, before being able to complete our mission.

After our fix we would find everything hilarious and laugh gleefully, egging each other on. But our high-spirited mirth would soon turn to derisive jeers from the more cynical voices in my head as I became increasingly incompetent and powerless to do anything without the use of cocaine.

Increasingly aware of my worsening financial straits, I decided to start dealing, and in spite of the recently introduced, draconian drug laws, at times carried fairly large quantities of the stuff through borders as well as openly puffing away on my coke ciggies. I shudder to think what could have happened, but back then it was just another day in my surreal movie in which nothing as crass as getting caught by the cops could ever happen to me.

Despite my lofty business ambitions, I never sold a grain of a gram, as every last crumb of powder went up my nose. The fiction I sold myself became more outrageous. I spent every last cent on coke and then in a final and desperate move, I offered my dealer my jewellery, not caring that I obtained a fraction of their actual worth in return. Anything for a few more lines.

At some point I crossed the line into paranoid psychosis and became convinced that the drug police were following me in order to get to my dealer. I was so convinced by these perceptions that I sought counsel from the infamous drug attorney of the day, who required payment in kind (a gram) before the consultation even started. This was surely confirmation that I was going insane. It really was the beginning of the end. And then after one last miserable weekend in the tiny kingdom, it was all over.

Broke, I had driven down to Swaziland, hoping to wheedle some free produce from my dealer. That weekend his family was away and I spent the next two days watching him processing powder cocaine while he exalted and expounded upon the rush and euphoria from smoking freebase crystals. His nose was damaged, a consequence of his extensive nasal use, which meant that snorting was out of the question, besides which he made it sound like sniffing was now for mere mortals and amateurs.

Thankfully, my guardian angels were looking out for me, because I didn't see the attraction. And despite the man himself showing me the ropes of smokeable coke, I never did experience the much-vaunted paradisiacal high.

Maybe it was something about the paraphernalia that made it seem common and well … too much like lying in a gutter with a needle in my arm for my liking. It's remarkable how I was able to make all these distinctions, but I'm grateful for my irrational snobbery; otherwise, knowing me, my addiction may well have taken a more sinister detour.

I returned home with a heavy heart, knowing that the glorious or perhaps ignoble love affair was finished. And as I began my grieving period, I was thrown into a morass of withdrawal symptoms and for the next month or so resembled a creature of the netherworld, barely human, as I battled to find the energy to stay alive.

I was working in public relations at the time, at a company

called Precious Imports and Exports. Precious had offices around the globe and was renowned for its Persian carpets, although it had diverse interests, from art and greyhound racing to computer software. Fortunately for me, the CEO of the company, who was as charismatic as he was an original, took a liking to me, which meant that my colleagues more or less left me to my own devices and didn't ask too many questions about my increasingly strange behaviour.

After that final trip to Swaziland, I would get to my office, which was sequestered from the main showrooms and art gallery, and just sit there for hours, cabbage-like, waiting for the day to end. One of my responsibilities was to churn out press releases and haul them around to various journalists. I managed to dredge up some puffery about the current art exhibition, if only to get the demanding diva of a curator, Madame Valkyrie, off my back, but even the thought of peddling this uninspired dross around town was way outside my myopic frame of reference. I binned the offending material, all the while grunting what I hoped would pass for vocal assurance that the deliveries had been completed.

Well, whoever said that 'It aint over 'til the fat lady sings' knew something about divas, as a few days later Madame Valkyrie stalked into my office. 'Joanna darrlink, there has been notthink yet about thees magneeficent paintinks?' Trying to appear interested, I naturally blamed the journalists for their failure to provide what was, after all, free publicity, as I shooed her out my inner sanctum, and fell back into my state of inertia.

It was a struggle even to breathe, and I dread to consider what I might have gone through had I been completely abstinent because, as pitiful as I was, I was somewhat shielded from complete cocaine rock bottom by my continued and liberal use of prescription drugs. After all, it was the big C that was destroying me, my other pills were fine, I told myself, which was probably my greatest self-deception during my entire career as an addict. 'I have stopped using street drugs,' I reasoned. 'I am not a junkie anymore. Everything is cool and, anyway, doctors give me my medication which I need.' Thus I made it okay for myself to carry on using for the next twelve years.

# 7

# The Dark Prince

After a few months coke-free, I started to feel a lot better. I had regained my independence and was ready to start life with a clean slate. At the same time, I was feeling a little unsettled, unsure of where I belonged. It wasn't long before I turned to habits of old, and shortly after moving into my new apartment I began traipsing a retinue of nameless and faceless men through my bed. In the back of my mind I knew this was not an ideal environment for my young son, but I rationalised my behaviour by convincing myself that because Darren didn't actually see these men, it was okay. Obviously it wasn't, even if they were extremely brief encounters. But quite frankly I could have convinced myself that the moon was made of green cheese if it would have served me in some way.

Straight after the sex, I would have a moment of lucidity and would ask my latest paramour to leave, whereupon I would drink copious amounts of alcohol to block out the guilt. Yet a few nights later I'd be trailing a new suitor. Truth be told, I could not resist the brief moments of comfort and affirmation these encounters provided.

Although I didn't feel the need to sleep with every male I came into contact with, I did need them to find me attractive. I would feel unlovable if they didn't respond to me sexually; unless they could confirm my desirability, they were of no value to me. I am sure that, because of my attitude, I must have deprived myself of some potentially good male friends. But I just had no idea how to relate to men other than sexually.

Today it is almost amusing to realise that I was objectifying men long before I understood what it meant to be treated as an object or could recognise the same thing happening to me. I felt powerful and heady in my sexual conquests, buoyed up by the admiration of whichever man I was pursuing. But this feeling was short-lived, as immediately after sex I would feel dirty and ashamed; disempowered. I could never ever make peace with that contradiction in terms; the feel of power preceding sex, the vulnerability after. I might have maintained this cycle of self-limiting behaviour indefinitely had it not been for the arrival in my life of Bared.

Bared was one of the main partners at Precious Import and Export and was based in Paris. Our CEO was busy restructuring the entire company locally and had called in Bared to help in this regard. Bared's speciality was Islamic art, but he also had a passion for European paintings. He had dark brown liquid eyes and nearly black hair quite severely cut, though one could see that, left to its own devices, it might well have had a wave or two! He had an aquiline nose, which was fitting as I saw him as a bird of prey, powerful and beautiful. His eyebrows were constantly raised in question and his mouth was beautifully sensual, although it could turn cruel in an instant. He always dressed in conservative Saville Row-type suits and designer label ties. He was a first generation Frenchman, his parents having emigrated from Armenia in about 1920. He never really spoke about them but I imagine that his heritage must have had some effect on his psyche, particularly his views on women, which were quite old-fashioned to say the least!

I was drawn to this man who, outwardly at least, appeared different from any of my usual choices of men – I had simply never met anyone quite like him. And so I fell in love, probably for the first time in my life. We had met once before, in Luxembourg, during a whistle-stop business trip to all the Precious offices in Europe, America and Canada. I had mentally registered an attraction but filed it away and thought no more about him. Apparently, the universe had other ideas, though, as it conspired to bring us together again a few months later, in Johannesburg. Ever the idealist, I believed this was the man I had been waiting for, my knight in shining albeit somewhat rusted armour. My Prince of Darkness, as I called him.

Initially Bared seemed impervious to my feminine wiles, but I was relentless in my determination to wear down his resistance. The fact that he was married and, to all intents and purposes, happily so, made no difference to me. On the contrary, I brainwashed myself into believing that it was better that he was married, that it suited me that way. I reminded myself, as countless mistresses before me had done, that at least I would never have to do his laundry, cook for him, darn his socks. I could have the best of both worlds; a stimulating lover and companion, and the freedom to live my life as I wanted. (Not that I wouldn't have traded for his wife's position in a second.)

By and by we became lovers, and for the first time in ages I felt happy to be alive. I was attracted to his passion and his larger than life aura. Wearing the blinkers of love, I was unable to discriminate between strength and domination, and was convinced that this was someone who could tame my wild spirits. What I couldn't have known then was that he would do more than tame me; he would control me to such an extent that I'd come close to losing myself.

One thing that Bared and I shared was a vision to start our own company, an art gallery based in Sandown. I was hugely excited to be leaving Precious and even though our new company, The Company, would stay closely connected to it, this was only at an international level. I was so relieved as I had had enough of the local MD and her husband, who ran the place like their own private kingdom.

We decided to specialise in impressionist and post-impressionist art from Europe, mainly France and Switzerland, because of Bared's connections there. The beechwood-panelled showroom looked more like a French salon; it glittered in gold and marble and exuded an air of wealth and prestige. It was perfect. We cleverly marketed ourselves by sponsoring a non-commercial exhibition of post-impressionist paintings from a museum in Geneva which toured the main local art museums for nine months prior to our commercial launch and opening. At the height of cultural isolation in South Africa, people were starved for a taste of the outside world and the exhibition was hugely successful.

In the early stages of our affair we were quite the dynamic duo. But there were cracks from the start. As my life started to revolve around Bared, I reinvented myself to win his approval. Out went alternative and in came elegant and understated as I performed an extreme makeover sans surgery, swapping buccaneer trousers and coloured hairsprays for Chanel-type suits and dresses complete with high-heeled Magli court shoes. I had become the Jackie O of curatorship, and Bared adored the new me.

One of my less shallow transformations during that period was that I became genuinely passionate about the art we were selling. It helped that the artists of these works were deceased, as this meant that the only prima donnas I had to contend with, aside from myself, were the doyens and cognoscenti of the French art world. And I'd always had a soft spot for the French. I had started travelling frequently to Paris and Geneva, and my French, which had been fair to start off, improved immeasurably. Undeterred by the arrogance and bad manners of the French, I slavishly imitated them down to their every gesture, taking pride in becoming more Parisian than the Parisians.

Breakfast was always coffee and a croissant in some noisy but vibrant sidewalk café and lunches were a slow and languorous affair with plenty of care taken over the food. I loved that about the French. Food was so important, and prepared with such passion, but the portions were manageable. And then there was always the cheese platter. I would thrill over a dripping Brie draped over piping hot French bread. What could be better?

Even better than the food was the Galeries Lafayette with its fabulous dome of glass and steel. Paris was the birthplace of the modern department store. In those years, what with all the sanctions in South Africa, shopping at the Galeries was like being in paradise. I would buy the sheerest, glossiest Yves Saint Laurent pantyhose which had the designer's initials embossed in gold or silver on the ankle. They cost a fortune but transported ones legs to another level; I was the envy of all my friends, colleagues and family. I'd always taken good care of my skin, having grown up using Esteé Lauder, but in Paris I graduated to La Prairie and for the next few years spent a small fortune on keeping away wrinkles that hadn't even started yet.

I remember once complaining to my PA about how sore my feet got from all the walking in my heels. Not to mention the fact that my shoes got ruined on the cobble streets. She remarked, 'But Jo, why don't you wear flatter shoes to walk in and then you can put your heels back on once you reach your destination?' Quelle horreur! Walk along the streets looking anything but my best? It was too absurd. No, I would rather suffer the indignities of the pain, and what if someone saw me? This was a constant concern in my life; What if someone saw me and I didn't look my best? It could be quite exhausting.

For a while Bared and I were blissfully content. But our relationship was much like the children's rhyme about the little girl who had a curl ('And when she was good she was very very good but when she was bad she was horrid'). It was not long before Bared started to show signs of jealousy and possessiveness. Typically, I saw this as proof of how much he loved me. At the same time, his feelings of envy triggered my own; I hated that he had a wife and resented any time he spent with her instead of me.

Bared demanded to know where I was at all times. Even when we were on opposite sides of the world, he would call and if, for example, I had popped out to buy a packet of cigarettes, for him this would be sufficient proof of my infidelity. If he perceived that another man so much as glanced in my direction, he would accuse me of having done something to provoke the look. I remember an incident at one of our gallery openings. I was talking to one of the guests, a very attractive young man, when I noticed Bared looking in our direction. His face had turned dark red in anger and his eyes were like iridescent jade as sparks flew out, burning me with their intensity. I felt angry and fearful simultaneously. Angry that I felt scared. Scared that I didn't know what he would do. He came over and said to the guest in a silky but dangerous tone, 'I hope that Jo is entertaining you properly.' Nobody was fooled, but not knowing how to respond, I just stood there grinning inanely while the guest mumbled something and slunk away. Later that evening, he harangued me about my flirtatious behaviour, on and on, ad nauseum, until eventually I apologised unconditionally and for a while things were okay. That was the pattern.

On the work front, at least, I was flourishing. I somehow managed to access a side of me that was able to put together exhibitions and to prepare the catalogues, which required countless hours of dedicated research and painstaking attention to detail. I thrived on the affirmation that success brought. But I had yet to achieve that elusive state of balance, and while I was doing well on the career front, the situation with Bared was beginning to wreak havoc on my psyche. Far from bringing security, as I'd initially thought he would, I found myself more insecure than ever, dependent on him for my raison d'être. The uncertainty of never knowing where I stood with him made me increasingly erratic. For example, if we were arguing long distance, I might, in a fit of pique, slam the phone down on him. Minutes later I would panic, freezing on the spot in the same way as my computer when it would not respond to any input from the mouse or keyboard. I would stand by the phone, unable to function until I had spoken to him again and 'made nice'. It didn't matter if I was supposed to be giving a lecture, meeting clients, going on television or had an appointment with the Pope himself; our secretary would find herself making excuses, delaying, postponing and sometimes cancelling altogether, while I attempted to track Bared down – not always an easy feat in the days of no cellphones or email. Sometimes, given time differences, conferences and, perhaps, karma, it could take days until I had spoken to him and felt that life was once again worth living.

Outwardly, Bared presented an image of the sophisticated but genuine, suave but chivalrous. A gentleman of honour, he made our clients feel comfortable, which was just as well since our artwork sold for anything in the region of a million rand, unheard of in those days. Silver-tongued and with the added benefit of his attractively accented English, punctuated now and again by the odd word in French, he was the consummate salesman and could close any deal. Even my mother, notoriously judgemental, doted on him because of his considerable charms and was quick to take his side in some of our more public clashes. But behind closed doors, as the saying goes, he could be far from charming. Once he went as far as to slap me in the face. It was the only time he ever got physical, but still I made it okay by telling myself that it was my fault because I had hit him first (which I had, out of sheer frustration ages into our screaming match). And when our next door neighbours came to see what was going on, I told them that everything was okay. I just wasn't ready to leave him then.

Lacking healthier coping mechanisms, sulking and shutting down became my weapon and major line of defence against his more insistent and articulately hostile offensives. Increasingly incapable of withstanding his vitriolic attacks, I would frequently flounce out of restaurants, once jumped out of a moving car at night on a busy highway and twice ran out of hotel rooms in strange cities to check myself onto a different flight to get away from him. One evening we were supposed to be attending a bar mitzvah dinner. We had been fighting all day – I can't remember exactly why, only that he had been exceptionally critical of me and I was a wreck – and I kept threatening not to go as I felt I couldn't deal with him anymore. 'You will come,' he told me in a flat voice.

'I'm not coming, Bared,' I answered in a pathetic tone, half crying.

He repeated himself, 'Jo, you will come, otherwise, I promise you, you will be sorry.'

I was already sorry, sorry for myself, and I knew that I would go. He left first and I agreed to meet him there. I dressed in an elegant black dress which I thought he would like. It was unusual for me in that it showed some flesh, but it still erred on the side of good taste. I arrived a bit late, went to our table and sat down. Within five minutes he snarled, 'What do you think you are wearing? Who are you looking to fuck tonight?'

The more I tried to placate him, explaining that 'I bought this dress for you', I was told what a 'fucking whore' I was, and eventually I ran out of the hall. I felt sure that people thought I was the one with the problem. After all, they saw me running out and behaving strangely while he, to all intents and purposes, appeared as suave and as calm as ever. I'm embarrassed to say that I went home and changed, went back to the party, and we acted as though nothing had happened. But I was heartbroken.

I always went back. I guess I felt that I couldn't live without him. I had become the archetypal victim, stuck in my powerlessness and growing ever more dependent on him. If he wanted something, he knew exactly what buttons to push and I was so eager to placate and please him that he knew he could get whatever he wanted. Like the time he decided he wanted to have a threesome, with me and another woman.

The cajoling began days before the event. When I refused, he turned it into an emotional harangue, 'After all Jo, it's not like you haven't done anything dirty before. What about that night in PE?' And here he cleverly and manipulatively hit on a sore spot. Some years before, when I'd still been working for Precious, I'd had sex with a client in order to sell him a very expensive Persian carpet. I made the mistake of telling Bared about it and he chose to fling it in my face as often as he could. 'You bastard,' I said. 'I'm not going to do it because of that shit. You can't keep throwing that in my face!' I continued to refuse and eventually he hit me with 'If you loved me, you'd do it.' Eventually, after hours of cajoling I gave in, but felt manipulated into doing something that I didn't want to do.

Bared scoured the papers looking for the 'right' person and eventually Anne-Marie came to the hotel room. She sat down and told us that this was her first night doing this and she was quite nervous. I have to admit that I was naive enough to believe her. Anyway, she and Bared got busy and I started to cry. For some reason, it really upset me, so I proceeded to drink and drink until I started to feel more relaxed, and by the time I got in the act I was surprised to find it almost exciting. After all, she was quite attractive; with her strawberry-blonde hair she looked like a pale version of a Titian model. She was voluptuous without being fat and her skin was incredibly soft. The fact that I rather enjoyed it in the end Bared found untenable, and after our ménage à trois he started to accuse me of being 'a lesbian dyke'. 'No man will want you,' he spat, with a degree of cruelty in his voice that I hadn't noticed before.

It was shortly after this incident, perhaps the final straw, that I found the courage to mutiny, albeit silently, as I was too intimidated to challenge him directly. It was the age-old dynamic of perpetrator meets abuser; I started refusing him sex. I would turn him down and then tell him that the only way he would get sex was if he did or got me what I wanted. I know this was pretty unevolved stuff, but it was the best I could do at the time.

Our relationship was more or less common knowledge; about the only person in the universe who might not have known with any degree of certainty about it was his wife, Nathalie. Bared, macho sadist that he was, took great delight in this on the few occasions we were all together for an extended period of time. I think it made him feel like a lord of the manor, having his wife and mistress at his side.

I remember when a party of us, including my son Darren, Bared's wife and both their kids plus a family from Durban, who were very good clients of ours, holidayed together in Juan les Pins-Antibes in the south of France. Sadly, my drug addiction was forging ahead largely unnoticed and about six days into yachting by day on the Med and rubbing shoulders with the glitterati in Cannes by night, I ran out of pills and promptly went into withdrawal. I didn't know exactly what it was but I knew enough to connect my being sick to not having my 'fix'. At first, I was unfazed. I didn't realise until later that codeine was a controlled substance, and as such, could not be purchased in over-the-counter medications. Desperate, I found a doctor, but he was only prepared to give me a few mild painkillers for my 'flu-like symptoms'.

I made an effort to act like all was well but there would be days when I simply could not keep up the pretence and go aboard the yacht. On those days I would leave my five-year-old boy in the care of Bared and the others while I went back to our holiday flat to suffer alone until evening. One afternoon, as I lay prostrate, I nearly had a heart attack as suddenly Bared was screaming and shouting outside the window like a complete lunatic. Not believing my story of being ill, and beside himself with his delusional jealousies, he was hoping to catch me in flagrante delicto. He seemed quite chastened to find me so sick and was over-compensatingly pleasant to me for the next few days.

I did manage some stunning highlights with Darren. I remember going to the beach with him and Bared and his kids. Darren adored Bared, who I must say was great with children, and I can still picture Darren on his shoulders as he took him out into the water. Darren loved the sea and those days on the beach were magical.

But one less pleasant memory haunts me to this day. It was one of those days when I couldn't face joining the others on the yacht and the withdrawals were particularly bad. That day I kept Darren with me. Desperate for something to alleviate the pain, I spent the whole day, from ten in the morning, walking up and down the streets of Juan les Pins, Darren in tow, while I searched for pharmacies. I have this image in my mind of Darren, so small and trusting, clutching my hand, patiently following me from one pharmacy to the next. Needless to say I couldn't get anything that I was looking for and I felt shattered. Later in the day, even in my single-mindedness, I realised that Darren was exhausted, and as much as he tried to keep up, never uttering a word of complaint, at last his little legs gave in and I had to carry him the rest of the way.

We left France soon after that and back home, sufficiently soothed by narcotics, I pushed aside the nightmarish aspects of the past couple of weeks, reframing the holiday as 'the time of my life!'

As the year lumbered on I was unable to keep pace with my mind, which was hurtling along at breakneck speed courtesy of the reappearance in my life of Ladymania. I became more frenzied as I sought perfection in the military-like execution of each new exhibition. Feeling increasingly worthless in my relationship with Bared, I relied on the admiration of others to make me feel better, and the ultimate experience was always our vernissage, typically a champagne and caviar affair in which no expense was spared in an effort to provide a luxurious backdrop to the richness of the paintings. Yet however successful the evening was, at some stage the saboteur in my head would snipe, 'If people only knew who you really were!' or, 'You're such a fraud' or 'You could have done better,' while I sipped on my Bollinger pink fizzy, hoping no one would see through my defences, as I searched for more compliments that would keep my rapacious hunger at bay.

It was very tempting to believe that I was the person these people claimed I was, through their praise and admiration. But like other things I was addicted to, this affirmation only went skin-deep, and when everyone had gone I would be left feeling despairing and deflated and once again looking around for the next 'hit' to take away my unfelt pain and disease.

Then, almost surprisingly, I turned thirty. Surprising because it was a landmark that for years I had publicly announced I would not be alive to celebrate. So I had lived to tell another tale, though it had started to feel like I was living on borrowed time. I had planned to meet Bared in Geneva to celebrate my birthday, but instead of being excited as I boarded the plane, my mood was a mix of anxiety, agitation and depression. Twenty minutes into take-off, I was swigging back a potent Molotov cocktail of red wine and sleeping pills to stave off my apprehension. It turned out I had good reason to worry.

Geneva was dismal. Bared and I disagreed on everything, the weather was awful and we fought constantly. With the clarity of hindsight, I believe I was looking for conflict, because this gave me an excuse to flirt with my self-proclaimed prophecy of dying and to seriously consider suicide. After Geneva we travelled to Vevey to meet up with another of the partners, the Maltese Falcon, so-called because he was originally from Malta and, like Bared, reminded me of a bird of prey. They even looked a bit alike, although The Maltese was more European with long hair and lighter eyes. He was shorter than Bared but his energy was equally powerful.

Besides being a colleague, The Maltese was also one of Bared's closest friends. They were synchronistic partners in that The Maltese was an economist and so they each had prodigious talents in different areas. He had an immense appetite for life, and like my designated namesake for him, he was a hunter of note, collecting people, places and things as the fancy took him.

The Falcon is also a symbol of hope to those in bondage, whether moral, emotional or spiritual, and so it's not surprising that I felt so close to him, and he soon became a trusted confidant. Since I was unable to be friends with a man without on some level sexualising the relationship, every now and then I would ask, 'So

Maltese, what about you and me?' And he would always confirm the mutual attraction, but fortunately kept relations between us at just the right mix of mild double entendres and genuine camaraderie, thus ensuring me a valuable ally.

He was certainly one of the shrewdest men I ever met, with an amazing clear-headedness, but he could also be ruthlessly intolerant, impatient and rude, and was not without a small amount of vanity. Although these qualities could be delightful and often amusing from a distance, it was a different story when he directed his wrath at you. I remember he had to travel unexpectedly to London and I was at his home when he phoned Brigid, his PA and girlfriend, to tell her what to pack and what arrangements to make. He was barking down the phone, 'And my passport is in the office safe …' when there was some interruption on the other end and suddenly he snapped, 'Don't you dare interrupt me, and I said it's in the safe!' This was followed by a pause as he opened the desk drawer in front of him. And there was his passport! When he told her he'd found it there was no a hint of apology in his voice. He was simply always right.

During our stay in Vevey it was World Cup Soccer, which meant that Bared and Maltese spent an inordinate amount of time huddling in front of the tube and behaving like football hooligans while I silently fumed, feeling neglected. At some stage during our stay, Maltese and I found time to talk, and in my own dysfunctional way I tried to ask for help by making oblique references to my mythology around having turned thirty. I knew that Maltese hated the way Bared treated me, which was a trump card that I liked to play to garner sympathy. Often, though, frustration would override pity when I would refuse to follow his advice and leave Bared. He could not understand my seeming addiction to chaos and pain.

Bared and I left for Paris and I made a last weak effort to express my desolation, but he seemed indifferent to my muted appeals. Paris might have been the City of Love but it was also the place where Bared and I were forced to separate as he went back to his home with Nathalie and I went to my hotel. As we parted ways at the airport, I felt overburdened by the tragedy of our star-crossed union. By the time I reached my hotel, I was immersed in a sea of hopelessness in which nothing mattered, life was meaningless and I convinced myself that my family and Darren would be better off without me.

It was in this state, what I call my 'untouchable space between two worlds', that, without any hesitation, I downed every single pill in my possession. Having learnt from my previous experiences of running out of meds, I had stocked up for this trip and probably had enough pharmaceuticals to put half of Paris to sleep. But as with my first attempt, the phone rang. It seemed that my earlier appeals to the Maltese had not been in vain, as through the candyfloss in my head I heard his voice on the other end of the receiver, 'I knew something was not kosher and had to call.' Yet again, I was saved by the phone.

I remember nothing of what followed, but it was evidently a melodrama of the highest order, with the Maltese orchestrating all the arrangements from Switzerland to Paris, right down to the detail of the American Hospital, a private clinic in the very posh suburb of Neuilly, where I awoke from a coma a day later. Apparently, while it was still touch and go as to whether I would survive, my dearly beloved Bared was beating his breast in sorrow, professing his undying love and calling the hospital every hour for the latest update. But once I was out of the woods, for the time being at least, he shifted into the refuge of the moral high ground and when he came to see me that afternoon, greeted me with 'Did you have to do this now? You know I spend every Sunday with my family.'

I have had the dubious distinction of having been depressed in four of the world's continents and, comparatively speaking, there are worse places to go through a dark night of the soul than the luxurious calm of a private room at the world-renowned medical centre wherein I found myself. But despite vast empathy shown to me by the professor of psychiatry there, I struggled to come to terms with my latest recklessness. Although attempting suicide was an extreme measure, I felt as though I had to push myself to the limit in order to make any kind of change, and I didn't know any other way to do this. I felt a bit like the legendary Phoenix and thought that I too could rise from the Ashes. For a time this would work in that after each attempt on my life I would feel it possible to rebuild and even get in touch with some gratitude about being alive. But unfortunately I was never able to maintain this; I struggled to find the emotional stamina necessary to grapple with the underlying cause of my actions. I suppose this is understandable – I had to be in a stronger place to deal with that.

Although I was advised to stay for at least a week to recuperate, Bared, resentful of how expensive this was going to be, was eager to get me released and hauled me out at the first opportunity, reminding me that we had urgent business in the south of France. I submissively followed his lead but not before obtaining a very large prescription with as much or maybe more drugs as I'd had before. After all, as I'd explained to the Prof, 'I'm so sad, I need them, and I promise I'll be careful.'

It's an interesting anomaly in France that without a prescription it is impossible to obtain anything addictive, but within the system, the French love their meds, or should I say that the doctors love to over-prescribe, and France is Europe's largest consumer of sleeping pills, tranquilisers and anti-depressants. So it was easy for me to walk away with plentiful supplies and I wasn't complaining. It was harder to convince Bared that I needed them. Whether his reluctance was out of concern for my wellbeing or his pocket is still unclear. I might have been passive in most areas of my life at the time, but when it came to my stash, I would have 'killed the bull'. Hence I bought my legal Smarties and we were on our way to Nice within the hour.

Perhaps in the top-drawer surroundings of wealth and prestige, it was easy to delude myself into thinking that my problems were high-class and genteel, and I colluded with Bared in pretending the incident never happened. But a line had been crossed and there was nothing high-class about the abuse that followed. It was as though Bared gave himself permission to punish me for all real and perceived sins, and the relationship deteriorated further.

I tried to leave him at least a dozen times but I just couldn't deal with the feelings of absolute emptiness that threatened to engulf me when I thought of leaving him, and so I took the line of least resistance and stayed. Bitter at being trapped in this situation, I lashed out by beginning a couple of mindless affairs with two of our very good clients. I revelled in how much it would hurt and injure Bared's sense of masculinity if he found out, but couldn't see how much what I was doing further disempowered me.

Looking back, I am able to see that this behaviour was partly a symptom of my mood disorder, as around this time Ladymania pulled me onto the floor for a marathon dance session. As I jitterbugged, boogied, whirled and finally breakdanced my way through the next months, I grew bored with the safety of the rarefied atmosphere of impressionism and post-impressionism that I lived and breathed. I developed a new obsession; to bring contemporary art to 'culturally starved' South Africans. Curiously, I encountered no opposition from Bared as I splurged wildly on a collection of art that said more about where I was at than any real response to a market need. From the visually disorientating, disfigured fringe collages of Jiri Kolar to the genderless, faceless nudes of Claude Garache to the surrealist comic strips of Valerio Adami, the artwork I chose reflected my unravelling sense of self. Our clients resisted our 'new look' quite vociferously, but, convinced this was the right path, I brushed off their criticism with all the zeal of the newly converted and instead lamented their 'ignorance'.

Commercially, the exhibition was not a success; nevertheless, I remained the darling of the media, who loved me for bringing something new into the stuffy art world. More and more I believed our own public relations and press propaganda about who I was. I was spending recklessly on other things, too. A few weeks before flying off to meet Bared for a reconciliation of sorts in Geneva, I waltzed into Schwartz Jewellers and, within minutes, purchased a

Piaget watch for about a hundred thousand rand. That night, in a moment of rare and brief clarity, I was shaken enough by what I'd done and pleaded with my mother to take the watch back – which fortunately she did, and I never asked what had transpired during the exchange; I felt too humiliated.

As if that wasn't enough to teach me a lesson, two days before leaving for Geneva, I impulsively and secretly bought a BMW 325. By the time I was sitting in first class Swiss Air I was too busy quaffing champagne and making eyes at Gold, my latest distraction, to worry about the car, and I relegated the thoughts to distant compartments of my mind.

I had been waiting at the airport when I noticed this man giving me the once over. We started chatting and discovered that we were on the same flight to Geneva, only I was travelling first class and he was travelling business class. So eager was he to continue our conversational foreplay that he got himself upgraded to first class.

I called him Gold because he was all about the money. He was probably the most unattractive man I have ever been involved with, and the least stable. The fact that I was oblivious to his lack of charm speaks volumes for my own state of mind at the time.

Quite aside from the bubbly, I was soaring so high that I'm sure I could have flown all the passengers to Switzerland on the strength of my manic mood. Gold and I flirted as we carried on the conversation we had started in the airport lounge, and by the time we arrived in Geneva I was in love, again, convinced that this was the man with whom I wanted to spend the rest of my life.

I went directly to the nearest phone and called Bared. 'I've met someone else,' I told him, made brave by my newfound love. 'Please don't come to Geneva.' He asked me a few questions and even asked to speak to Gold, and then that was that. I called Johannesburg and broke the 'happy tidings' to my shocked family and informed them that they should not try to get in touch with me but that I would be home within a few weeks.

Gold was a professional gambler; he played blackjack for a living, which would account for why the two of us were attracted to one another in the first place. The next ten or so days went by in a merry-go-round of Manhattan doubles, which became my drink of choice, and decadent living in a suite at the Château de Divonne, a nonpareil of elegance and grace with its exquisite formal gardens and parkland. Every evening was a formal black-tie occasion in the casino, and because gambling seemed to be the one and only vice that thankfully didn't interest me, it gave me the time to people gaze while Gold spent hours at a time staking his bets.

I was in heaven; if I'd only been grounded enough to really appreciate it! But with Ladymania in residence, it was a fairytale based on lies. For the Joanne hobnobbing with the glitterati on the casino floors was not the real Joanne. Rather, it was another of my numerous identities in residence, this time Laurence.

Don't get me wrong. I was not suffering from multiple personality disorder, or as it is called today, dissociative identity disorder, but I was so fragmented and broken that there were definite and distinct parts of me, for which I consciously chose different names. Laurence was my inner Parisian. I had always been a card-carrying Francophile and was a sycophant to Parisian arrogance. Laurence was the manifestation of that part of me, conjured up from years of enthusiastic devotion. Self-assured, sophisticated, and sensual without being vulgar, she was also witty and could make small talk with the best of them. She could be quite exhibitionistic and secretly thrilled at being noticed and perved over by the men as she strutted her stuff. Laurence was me, but a manic, unrealistic version thereof.

I was so animated and high that my behaviour bordered on reckless. At the casino there was a group of very serious looking players from Libya who, each night, opened their own table with different ceiling rates to the rest of the patrons. One evening, with the self-aplomb that came from being Laurence, I inveigled my way into their party and was about to spend some one-on-one time with a rather dashing man when suddenly I remembered that I had a flight to catch. I'd been so engrossed that I'd completely forgotten

I was leaving that night, and almost didn't make it to the airport on time. I have often wondered if they would have been quite so amicable and familiar had they known my true (Jewish) identity lurking behind my facade of cosmopolitan 'world traveller'. Happily I never had to find out.

My dalliance with Gold was short-lived as, on my return from Switzerland, I couldn't believe what I had gotten myself into and I would look at him thinking, 'Well Jo, this time you really have outdone yourself!' Apart from his less than attractive features, he lived in a state of constipation (both physically and emotionally) and travelled around with this enormous enema bag, which he used every day. It was revolting. Returned to my senses at last, I extricated myself as quickly as possible.

It is said that revenge is a dish best served cold, and my life was about to become decidedly chilly as Bared, following in the best traditions of Machiavellianism, schemed for weeks behind the scenes and finally managed to manoeuvre me out of the business.

A few months previously, in a fit of pique and in an attempt to punish him, I had handed him a letter stating my wish to resign – though I had no intention of following this through. It was all part of our game. I thought the matter had been forgotten, but Bared had also very cleverly managed to get me to sign documents which to all intents and purposes lost me my directorship. He put it in some crafty way, explaining that he wanted to protect me in case of some or other eventuality. After the whole Gold affair, all he had to do was to haul out this letter along with the one about my resignation.

It was such a stroke of masterful deviousness. Even though it was not strictly legal, I was in no state to contest anything, and that was the end of a glorious era. I'd been hoisted by my own petard.

I think my family felt it was no more than I deserved, so there was no sympathy to be had there, and I sank into a morass of despair. Yet, despite everything that happened, a few months later I went back to him. Where else was I going to go? He made sure that

I knew that he was doing me a great favour in taking me back and savoured every moment of my humiliation and his victory. Back in his life but not in the business, I was out in the freezing cold like a beggar with my nose pressed up against the glass pane of a past life. It was unbearable, but I didn't yet know about letting go and surrendering, so I resigned myself and gave up.

# 8

## *Getting shrunk*

Over the years I had a largely co-dependent relationship with psychiatrists, many of whom were more like private merchants than mental health professionals. Looking back, it is clear that I was drawn to the shrinks who themselves had issues, and that there was not a whole lot of therapy going down in their offices. But of course I was there for the drugs, not the therapy, so whatever quirks I had to put up with were a fair trade, or a bit of horse trading. Either way, we each got our needs met.

I was never keen on seeing psychologists – not that I hadn't been counselled and over-analysed by umpteen serious-looking therapists from every school of psychotherapy available over the years. Part of the reason this type of therapy had such little impact on me was because, from a young age, I was able to mastermind most sessions in order to have the shrinks earnestly believe that they were making progress with me. I had huge trust issues and I wasn't about to simply put my life into the care of these people, as nice as some of them appeared to be. I learnt to answer their questions in such a way that they were convinced of my compliance and their success. This ability to deceive was one in which I took perverse pride. But the main reason I was reluctant to see these therapists was not due to any lack of constructive breakthroughs into my psyche; it was based strictly on what I perceived to be their major handicap, and one for which there was no levelling the field – they were simply unable to prescribe medication. Why would I bother?

Instead I turned to psychiatrists, of which many were more than accommodating when it came to supplying my fixes. First there was Dr Chill, a rather bland if self-satisfied little man who hid a frosty heart and eyes that registered dollar signs behind a broad smile purporting to be both welcoming and helpful. I wasn't fooled by the ingratiating smirk, but he offered an irresistible prize; once a month he would put his million dollar signature on a script for the love of my life, Valoron. As I've previously explained, I would have done almost anything to get those exquisite red beauties, and because I was using way more than the scheduled dose, I needed as many doctors as possible to write out scripts.

Valoron is a Schedule 7 medication. From Schedule 3 upwards, one needs a script, but one can get a repeat on the script for up to six months, and it is also possible to have it telephoned and faxed through to the pharmacist. However, for Schedule 6 and 7 meds one needs the original prescription in one's hot little hand – no photocopy or repeat will be accepted. These are serious narcotics we are talking about. But Dr Chill was more than happy – well maybe happy is overstating, let's say obliging – to put pen to paper as long as I paid for a session. I didn't even have to see him; I could collect my 'envelope' from reception. And so our Faustian bargain was struck. Even though I knew it wasn't kosher, I had sold my soul for considerably less in the past, so I viewed it as a good deal, and we carried on our 'Let's pretend to have a therapeutic relationship' charade for over a year. That is until I performed one of my more memorable suicide stunts and actually needed him in a real crisis, at which point he became mysteriously unavailable. That got rid of me very quickly.

Then there was Dr No. Stooped and cadaverous, with his hair all over the place, Dr No was the quintessential mad professor. He had an odd voice – deep on the one hand and nasal on the other, it was annoying to listen to. Dr No's speciality was narcotherapy, which basically meant conducting psychotherapy using narcotic drugs to induce a state in which the patient becomes more relaxed and communicative. There is no doubt in my mind that he perverted and hijacked this technique for his own personal satisfaction. Obsequious by nature, I think he felt powerful only when his patients were out of it. And he clearly enjoyed the 'compliant and amenable' space that the meds created.

He would give me shots of Valium mixed with something else, possibly Ritalin, but more probably a barbiturate. I certainly wouldn't have turned down any drugs, but the dose he gave me never really touched sides – a result of my tolerance levels and the fact that he gave me the complete heebie-jeebies, so to be vulnerable around him was completely out of the question. Once the session began, he would become quite animated, which was strangely at odds with his normally flat and inhibited personality. He'd begin to ask personal questions, which, as a psychiatrist, was understandable; but, difficult though it is to explain, there was something inappropriate and unprofessional in the phrasing of these questions, the way they seemed to manipulate you into giving him the answers he wanted.

But I needed his scripts, so I submitted to his ministrations for a while, until eventually it became too weird even for me, and after one session in which he spoke almost exclusively, and obsessively, about his wife, I left rather abruptly. I shudder to think of what else might have gone down under the guise of psychotherapeutic intervention. I already thought of myself as his experiment and I am not sure how far he would have gone had I stayed longer.

Then there was Dr Moribund. His offices were situated in downtown Joburg, in a dilapidated old building, on the bottom floor of which was a pharmacy – how appropriate. An old family business, or so it seemed, it was out of sync with what was happening to the town at that time, with most businesses having moved north. It was a strictly no-questions-asked type chemist, which was exactly what I needed, and from time to time, if desperate, I could always coax a few pills from them without a script. For the right price, obviously.

To get to his office you climbed into what seemed like the prototype elevator, which slowly and noisily creaked its way up to the eighth floor. Then it was down a dingy passageway, into his teeny rooms where you were faced by Mrs Moribund who also acted as his somewhat fierce secretary. I don't think that this is what she had envisaged for her life, sitting in depressing rooms where nothing matched, from the puke green filing cabinets to the apologetic yellow curtains, administering to the flotsam and jetsam of addicts and alcoholics who mostly made up his patients. I always psyched myself to be especially polite and friendly to her because she had power not only over his appointment book but also what he wrote in the scripts. I had gotten his number from Pete the journo, one of the gang from the good old coke days, and it certainly was one of my most prized referrals ever.

I was never quite sure of Dr Moribund's story. I knew there had to be one, and with my usual flair for the dramatic, I made up all kinds of romantic explanations as to why this rather shy and self-effacing man had ended up in a dingy hole in the middle of Joburg, generously dispensing death to the addicted population. I once thought I smelt alcohol on his breath,. but the ordinariness of alcoholism seemed too banal an explanation for his situation. At that stage I didn't regard alcohol as an addictive substance, anyway. (Nor did I acknowledge that the pills I was taking were drugs or that I was an addict.)

Of course what concerned me was not so much his personal affairs as what he was able to give me. Each month, he would offer up a smorgasbord of pharmaceuticals. For a greedy little gourmand like myself, it was like ordering from a self-help menu of medicine. If it was available, I could have it, and this is how those little red devils, Seconal, first came into my possession. Seconals were barbiturates, which were the predecessors of benzodiazepines. It was only later that the addictive potential of barbiturates was realised, encouraging researchers to look for new classes of sedative-hypnotics. The potency of the barbs made them extremely dangerous if abused, and clearly I was abusing them!

There was nothing subtle about the pills' ability to deaden the most persistent and intrusive of thoughts and feelings. And as a soporific, they could be relied on when taken in conjunction with all my other sleeping potions. Given that the difference between a sedating dose and a dose that could kill was so small, it's quite surprising that I didn't die of an accidental overdose (let alone all my more deliberate attempts).

Each time I left Dr Moribund's rooms clutching my precious piece of paper I felt as though I'd won the lottery. I would usually fill out the script at one of the pharmacies in town where it was less likely that any questions would be asked. At my local haunts, eyebrows would definitely be raised, not only at the quantities but also at the dosages. So I avoided suspicion by patronising different chemists in various other suburbs around Johannesburg.

At this stage, I was taking so much Valoron that at certain times of the day I wouldn't be able to talk properly and the one corner of my mouth would droop down and freeze in a Bell's palsy-type position. Not even the horror of being unable to control my facial muscles was enough to stop me, though. I was surprisingly philosophical in accepting it as the price that I had to pay to maintain my zombie state. The most important thing was that I felt nothing; this was the absolute bare minimum for my survival, and I would go to almost any lengths to achieve this state.

I continued in this way for some time, until the delicate status quo gave way and even I could no longer pretend that everything was okay. I made several more attempts to kill myself, and many of these should have finished me off, but time and time again I was rescued at the last minute.

At some point I added razor blades to my arsenal, and the ceremony became more gruesome. The ritual was always the same; I would swallow as many pills as I had and then descend into a warm bath whereupon I would get to work with my trusty blade. I had read enough books wherein the heroine slit her wrists and died within minutes. The reality for me proved to be somewhat different. Firstly, I was cutting the wrong way, in the wrong direction, and I wasn't about to hit my artery any time soon. A minor detail the books had neglected to mention. Nevertheless I found the cutting to be quite cathartic. I would lie in the bath, hold my arm and literally push the blood out, and as I watched the life force flow out of me, I would float away and everything would feel okay in my little world. It was as if time slowed down, even stopped for a while; I felt at peace. The cutting and resultant scars externalised some of my internal issues.

I was not your average self-harmer in that I only ever cut in the context of a formal suicide mission. But once I'd started I would carry on carving my flesh quite wildly, all the way up my arm, always hoping to bleed enough to extinguish my life. I felt that being in the water allowed the blood to flow more easily, and I would keep squeezing, hoping to make it go even quicker. It has always astonished me that in my so-called normal state, the sight of blood makes me feel quite queasy, but in those other spaces, it almost took on magical properties in its ability to make me feel better.

I felt no pain as I continued to butcher my arms; quite the opposite, as the neurotransmitters flooded my brain with natural opioids, leaving me feeling calm and composed until I passed out. It was only later when the medics were stitching up the unholy mess that it would hurt like hell.

I gouged deeply and always needed loads of stitches; and nothing annoys emergency doctors more than having to sew up a self-confessed cutter who has also taken bottles of pills. They would refuse to give me local anaesthetic in the hope of teaching me a lesson. Well, I was the queen of self-punishment, and if I hadn't yet mastered any lessons, I seriously doubted that I was going to learn anything from being punished by a few anonymous professionals.

Things deteriorated to such an extent that my mother and sister decided that I needed 24-hour surveillance, as they rightly felt that I could not be trusted after one particularly bad week when I tried three times to end it all. My memories of that week are all a bit blurred, which is probably not a bad thing, but I still have the only suicide letter that I ever wrote, before one of my worst attempts. I planned this attempt thoroughly, or so I thought. My mother and Phil were going to be out for the whole day, Darren was going to Ros, his grandmother on Stephen's side. And Elias, our housekeeper, was off for the day. I locked my bedroom door and shook thirty Seconals out of the bottle and swallowed them. I felt quite peaceful as I waited for them to take effect. The next thing I remember is waking up in ICU strapped down to the bed and hearing voices that were definitely not my own, nor apparently anybody else's from this world. I was completely psychotic. What I hadn't or couldn't have bargained on was Elias coming back and becoming suspicious when he saw my car but got no response from me when he tried to call me outside my room.

What I scribbled sums up quite clearly my state of mind at the time.

*Before I say anything let me just say that I really believe that this was inevitable for me. It really was just a question of time. Christ I'm tired but you see me now as I am without my 'glittering image'. I am completely exposed. But unfortunately underneath, there is nothing to take its place. There is no other image of anything else, only an empty shell. And I get angry and say why me? Why was I so flawed? Why could I never believe or trust in myself which results in all the pretence and the lies and the trying to live up to my 'glittering image'... I was never good enough, never clever enough, never anything enough. I constantly made the same mistakes ... I went blindly on making the wrong choices until finally it becomes too late and you run out of choices ... And then the glittering image is removed and I look in the mirror and I don't recognise what I see ... And then like a flash of lightning I see my life as maybe it could have been. And finally I am just very very sad ... So you see the games, the charades, the pretence, the dreams are finally over. So too are any hopes that I might have had of living a normal real life ... Ironic isn't it? That me, the master manipulator ended up being totally manipulated and outmanoeuvred by none other than herself or rather myself ... You all know that Darren was the only constant in my life, the only pure emotion that I ever had. I'm sorry if this doesn't make sense but it's so hard to say what I feel. And now I ask a favour and really my only request and it is to Ca. Ca, my sister, you are the godmother of my child. Please both now and in the future please tell him how much I loved him and that I know that he will have a wonderful life ... I will always be there with him ... Oh Christ how difficult this is ...*

I persuaded myself that my son knew nothing about these near-fatal acts, but of course I had underestimated the natural intelligence of little people generally and his intuitiveness in particular, and despite my wearing long sleeves at all times, he knew. Besides, there were only so many reasons one could give for my constant hospitalisations. Years later he told me that if I had succeeded in one of my suicide attempts, he would have killed himself as well. The reality of that continues to haunt me.

It was around then that I lost custody of Darren and he was forced to go and live with his father and his new wife, who, it must be said, was the epitome of the wicked stepmother. On a rational level I understood that I was incapable of looking after myself, let alone a vulnerable eight-year-old, but emotionally, I thought everyone was against me. In the pathetic condition that I was in, it was obvious that Stephen would win a custody case against me, but unbeknown to me, both Ca and my brother Richard signed affidavits stating that I was an unfit mother. God knows it was the truth but it stung coming as it did from my own family. Thus I used the situation as it another convenient excuse to feel sorry for myself and to be unable to get my act together, allowing me to carry on my dissolute lifestyle a while longer.

I didn't know how to live, and apparently nor did I know how to die. It was a psychic checkmate. And it was during this impasse that I found myself lying on the proverbial couch of Dr Feelgood, fourteen months before landing up in rehab.

Of the long list of shrinks that I consulted, Dr Feelgood was undoubtedly the most notable, or should that be notorious. I saw him at least twice a week, became completely dependent on him and sought his approval constantly. It would be some years before I could appreciate on any meaningful level that he had represented my father, and the concept 'transference'. Then, all I was able to divine was that I needed to please him, and if I did then he would give me drugs.

During my time with him, I continued to regress and became more and more out of control. One day I fell asleep at home with a lit cigarette and set my apartment alight. In addition to the financial insurance payout (I lied about the cause of the fire), I received a brand new Dunhill lighter. Dr Feelgood smoked – the two of us would puff away during my sessions like two conspirators – and in an effort to ingratiate myself with the good doctor, I presented him with this gleaming, shiny lighter. It was my non-verbal declaration of 'Take me – I'm yours'. And he did – take the lighter, I mean!

It was earlier in that year that I had first started to seriously entertain the idea of prostitution. And where else would I take my latest brainchild but to my guru? I explained to him my rationalisations and justifications for wanting to prostitute myself. Amazingly, he seemed to validate this decision, and so I began hooking at an escort agency called The House. I would bring all the graphic and salacious details to our sessions and from that point any pretence that our sessions weren't more about sex than the inner workings of my head dissolved.

It was in my nature to attempt to seduce and sexualise. It's what I knew. But as the months went by this twisted situation became increasingly harmful. Predictably, Ladymania (still untreated) then paid a visit, and as my spirits rose to the occasion of the dance, I informed Dr Feelgood about my plans to open up my own brothel. As part of my pitch I used words like distinctive, radical, unparalleled, elite, innovative, pioneering and similar superlatives to describe how supercalifragilisticexpialidocious it was all going to be. Incredibly, the doc excitedly participated in my 'enthusiasm' and told me about one of his more traumatised clients who he thought might be a perfect young hopeful for the business. I was exuberant and, disregarding confidentiality, he provided her name. I knew who she was instantly and was swept away in my aberrational dream world of visions which fortunately fell away after my dancing partner left the building. Thank goodness I never tried to contact her because she could only have complicated my life further. I had more than my share. But this all happened after my stint at The House, so I need to backtrack to the beginnings of my life as a 'working girl'.

# 9

# The House

It was 1993. I was 38 years old and half-heartedly looking for employment. Every morning I would dutifully buy *The Star* and browse through the classifieds. But instead of the ads for PR and gallery jobs, my eyes would keep drifting to the section with the ads that read 'Earn up to R25 000 pm in upmarket men's club'.

I think that I was always secretly fascinated by the world of prostitution. To me it seemed glamorous, alluring. And familiar. After all, sex was what I'd been trading in for most of my adult life, if I considered the countless one-night stands, seven-day wonders and myriad anonymous, and mostly mindless, sexual encounters.

One afternoon intrigue triumphed over any good sense that I may have possessed, and I took a deep breath and called the number, for one of these clubs, making an appointment for an interview the very same day – before I lost courage. Following the directions I'd been given, I drove north down Rivonia Road. For once, the voices in my head were quiet, almost as if they'd been stunned into silence at my latest adventure. I was grateful for the stillness – I was nervous enough as it was.

What felt like hours later, but was more like twenty minutes, I arrived at The House. I was met at the door by the inimitable Mr Larry Edwards. He was bald headed, quite good looking and probably in his mid-thirties. Charming and urbane, he seemed almost above an establishment like this, but I was soon to discover that his looks were misleading. I remember one night when a couple of girls were fooling around with each other – nothing explicit – and Mr Edwards had stood there surveying his fiefdom, so to speak, rubbing his hand repeatedly over his burgeoning erection.

Apparently all the prostitutes had 'stage names'. When Larry asked me what I wanted to be called I hesitated for a moment, wondering whether I should go with Laurence, the name I had used on meeting Gold. But as self-assured and sophisticated as Laurence was, I felt I needed something more suited to the occasion. And so I came up with Paris (and this was long before the days of Paris Hilton, or certainly before her days of sex-tape infamy! There must be something about the name …).

Paris was flashier than Laurence and her energy was unashamedly yet quite toxically sexual. She enjoyed being thoroughly sinful and thrived on titillating both men and women. And, convinced that they added to her mystery, she smoked Russian Sobranie cigarettes through a long, phallic, black and silver art deco cigarette holder.

In congruence with her imago, Laurence puffed away on the equally strong but more feminine coloured versions. They were foul and disgusting but looked the part, and in my world, appearance was everything. A box of coloured Sobranies came with a mixture of cigarettes – five different hues, four of each. I would buy three or four cartons at a time, open each packet so that I could colour code them and then, for example, repack twenty pink ones to a box, and so on. The pink lacquer shade was my favourite and became a hallmark of my hedonistic lifestyle. Indifferent to the extravagance and wastefulness, I discarded the others regardless of their brilliant shades. This act mirrored my own life of lavish self-destruction, but I lacked the capacity to see the connection.

That afternoon Larry explained everything thoroughly. The business operated on shifts, and there were levies that needed to be paid daily before you earned a cent. So, in other words, you paid to work. I forget the exact amount, but I think it was about R500 per shift. And the clients were charged a fixed rate of R250. After you had paid your levy, you kept any monies earned. But one had to keep in mind that you booked your shifts for the week ahead. One week I got measles and couldn't work my shifts, but was still made to pay my levies, and so ended up actually losing money! I am sure that those who had been there longer managed to negotiate better arrangements both as far as the fee structure was concerned and in terms of the shifts. I am not sure how many clients the others saw, but I only ever had a maximum of five clients a day.

Larry invited me to stay for the afternoon to get a feel for the place and to introduce me to a few of the 'girls', most of whom were much younger than me. There was the exotic-looking Leanne, who had long black hair and the lithe body of an uncoiled snake. She was dressed in a microdot skirt, ballerina pumps and a bikini top. Leanne and I would become friends, often teaming up to do threesomes. With my short, gelled back hair and androgynous look, we were a good complement for one another.

Then there was Trixie with her Marilyn Monroe hairstyle and a short one-piece in white stretch material which showed off every inch of her body. I was also introduced to the blue-eyed girl of The House, Colette. Word had it that she had bought property with her earnings from The House and that she had various other investments. I didn't know whether to admire her or to hate her, so I did both! I respected her for having done so well but I resented her for being so aloof. Thankfully most of the girls were quite friendly and open to me, but I felt quite out of place in my formal black pants suit and moderately heeled court shoes. (What does one wear to an interview when the job description is 'hooker'?)

I remember thinking that none of it seemed real, and beginning to feel like I was the protagonist in a Fellini movie. When I was in my teens, I belonged to the Johannesburg Film Society which met once a month in Rosebank to see the art movies of the day. I didn't always understand many of the avant-garde offerings but it was considered de rigueur to attend. The experience of watching those movies was not too dissimilar from how I felt on the afternoon of the interview; despite how surreal it was, how beyond my understanding, I knew I was going to see it through anyway. Looking back it's hard to believe I was so bold, or maybe I was just insane. Of course I was also aided and abetted by my co-conspirator, Dr Feelgood. I know that this misadventure was not his fault and I don't blame him. Especially because I'm convinced that I would have become a lady of the night regardless of his influence. It just saddens me that I never heard another point of view.

The ambience inside The House was chilled – it felt almost like a hotel or restaurant. There were several chefs in residence who served up meals to cater for the clients' every whim, from French cuisine to exotic curries to simple salads. And there was always plenty of alcohol available for both clients and staff. It was spacious inside and tastefully lit with low lights and standing lamps. Heavy oriental rugs were scattered across the floor; I remember how luxurious they felt beneath your feet.

As I sat there that afternoon I chatted to Kim, a tiny girl who would also become one of my friends. She was beautiful, if a bit hippy (I would notice that), and had been hooking for about a year. After a while she said, 'You see that guy over there?' I looked to where she was pointing and saw a fine-looking Indian man in a white suit right out of a Merchant Ivory production. She told me, 'He wants to meet you to do business with you.' My heart lurched as she explained to me that Rajesh liked to sleep with the new girls. He came over to our table and we started chatting. I told him that I was nervous, and as if this was his cue, he responded by suggesting that he 'take me through'. He led me to a room which I never saw again during my months at The House. As I undressed, my thoughts were going wild and I felt exposed and frightened, but thankfully he wanted only so-called missionary-style sex, so my intro to hooking was very genteel and civilised. Maybe that's what he did? 'Broke in' the new girls. And when he handed my R250, I thought, 'What could be easier?' I was sold.

I went home that evening full of the joys of spring with my first shift already booked for the following night. The next morning as I sorted through my wardrobe, I realised I would need to do some shopping. Finding the right sort of clothes proved to be easier than I'd expected. From a well-known shop in Rosebank, I bought a pair of shorts made from a mixture of velvet and velour and decorated in brightly coloured stones in blues, pinks, reds and yellows. They were spectacular. Horribly expensive, but then I reminded myself of the expression, 'If you want to make money you must spend money.' I wore them with black tights and high-heeled black boots. I also bought a pair of Levi jeans decorated with mother of pearl, which I turned into shorts! A number of the girls wore lingerie at work but I really couldn't bring myself to do that. It wasn't really my style, or should I say Paris's.

If clothes were fun and easy to find, shoes were nearly impossible. It wasn't like today when high heels are all the rage. The shoes then were more subdued and I really had to hunt to find extra high heels. What further limited my choices was the fact that I wouldn't wear open-toed shoes. I had and have a thing about toes being visible, so they had to be closed shoes.

The next evening I drove to work, anxious but excited – it felt like I was going to a party. I was wearing my lucky white shirt, a long silk button-up with pearl beads adorning the top half and a pair of gold aerobic tights which made my legs look magnificent. I arrived at work and thankfully saw Kim who showed me to a locker where I could leave anything I didn't want to carry around. I then moved through to the lounge area where we were expected to talk to the men and serve them drinks. This was helpful because it made things a little less intimidating and business-like.

On that first night, I spoke to Etienne, who apparently fell in lust with my legs at first sight. As he sat there he kept saying, 'Are they mine?' and I would answer, 'Of course', all the time thinking 'What planet is he on?' He proceeded to stroke my legs obsessively until I decided it was time to consummate this encounter. Off we went, and it was then that my glamorous illusion was nearly shattered.

Up until that point I had been able to delude myself that I was this elegant, high-class purveyor of sensual delights. But this room, and what happened in it, brought home the less palatable reality; I am a prostitute who fucks men for money. It was an awful, office-like cubicle with a massage bed and decor best described as seedy. As I took my clothes off, I had to keep reminding myself of the money. Once naked, Etienne asked, 'Please, Paris, can you walk up and down so I can see your legs?' So I did, while he went on mumbling 'Are they mine?' and I thought to myself, 'Does he not know that this is a fantasy?' But that was the whole point. It was the fantasy that would keep him coming back time and time again, as he became one of my regulars.

I struggled sometimes between the fantasy and reality of what I was doing. One night a group of young men came in; I could tell they were Jewish and I started chatting to one of them. After a while, I told him I was Jewish. He was a bit shocked, as in 'Oh my God, are there really Jewish prostitutes?' but then became quite understanding, or so I thought, naively. He seemed to like me and so we made a 'date' for the next night. When he didn't turn up I was really upset. I felt rejected and ashamed.

Yet a paradox prevailed. As distasteful and degrading as it all was, I loved the fact that men paid for the privilege of having sex with me. It made me feel worthwhile. And I must say that every time a man chose me over one of the younger girls I felt validated as a person. That I had to provide sex in order to get my needs met was just one of those things. After all, I was good at anonymous sex; it was intimacy that I had a huge problem with.

I learnt a few invaluable lessons early on in my life as a working girl. The first was how to put on a condom with my mouth. This was a really useful party trick. Under the guise of giving my client a blowjob, the condom would be on within seconds, resolving the issue immediately. It is amazing how many men do not want to wear protection and will even offer to pay more for this indulgence, and perhaps thrill, of playing Russian roulette with their lives.

There was another more personal reason why this slick and artful technique really worked for me. It meant that I didn't have to touch a man's penis. For years, I had had this aversion; I could not bear to handle a man's penis. When faced with the inevitability of getting down and dirty, I would start to feel sick and zone out immediately. Clearly, this was a bit of a handicap (no pun intended) for an aspiring prostitute. But the party trick solved that. And, of course, my prodigious use of drugs and alcohol helped me switch off enough to cope with what I had to do without feeling too traumatised.

As for the phobia itself, for years I had harboured a secret which at the time I believed partially explained my aversion to the male member. At the age of seven, I started piano lessons and, according to my teacher, was quite talented. In pursuit of what was probably more my mother's dream than my own aspirations to become the next Daniel Barenboim, I would walk up the road to Mrs Mayer for my hour of musical discipline, twice weekly. Then it was still considered 'safe' for children to roam the streets unescorted. After all, this was the mid-1960s and Verwoerd was still very much alive and firmly in charge of our South African Reich.

One day, en route to my regular class, a yellow Volkswagen Beetle stopped close to me and a man's voice beckoned me over. Being a polite and well-mannered girl, I complied, and he asked me for directions somewhere. He had his penis out his trousers and was playing with himself while talking to me. I remember the sheer mortification I felt as I stood there, frozen in shock.

My belief, even up until fairly recently, was that nothing else happened, and I told no one about this violation, not even my mother and Johnnie. I was sure that they would not believe me. So I blocked out the incident and, like most of my childhood memories, it was relegated to the buried recesses of my mind, only to come out in distorted forms throughout my life. It did have one immediate effect, though. I stopped going to piano lessons. I can't remember the excuse I invented, but predictably, my mother attributed my lack of enthusiasm to laziness.

It was then that I really began to self-soothe and medicate with food. One night, after a major binge on hamburger, chips and double milkshake at the local steakhouse, The Longhorn, I was rushed off to hospital where I had to undergo an emergency appendectomy. A hideous and appalling scar bears testimony more, I hope, to the urgency of the moment than to the skill of the surgeon. The family legend has it that I starting piling on the pounds after that. I bought into this story, as though there had been something bewitching about the operation. I now know better.

What I know now is that something more did happen (which goes a long way to explaining my peculiar aversion). I got into the car and was induced to touch the man's penis and masturbate him. I can remember feeling very bad, as though I was to blame. I obviously didn't yet know about the earlier abuse and, once again, I took on shame that wasn't mine, becoming more convinced than ever that I was intrinsically damaged and dirty.

The second lesson the other prostitutes taught me was how to have sex with your period. I had never seen my moon time as sacred, so shoving a sea sponge inside me in order to continue 'business as usual, darling' seemed ingenious. It's only in retrospect that I am able to see what a violation it actually was.

When the girls taught me these tricks of the trade I felt honoured to be accepted. It gave me a sense of security to know that I fitted in and belonged, albeit to a community exiled and marginalised by mainstream society. Unlike when I was with my own family, amongst these women I did not feel like the odd one out. Speaking of family – there's no doubt that mine knew what I was doing, but they chose to accept my 'I'm a hostess in a club' prevarication. It was rather like the 'elephant in the living room' that everyone ignores. I know that they were all appalled and horrified at what I was doing and did their tsk-tsking to each other about how truly disturbed I was. But no one spoke to me about it. That is how we operated in my family. We spoke about each other, behind one another's backs, and found it difficult, if not impossible, to be direct.

In the beginning I revelled in being so rebellious and so bad. I had recently discovered the new-age book *You Can Heal Your Life* by Louise Hay, which incorporated the power of visualisation and affirmations. Even then the book resonated, resulting in me asserting, 'I, Paris, am the best hooker in town!' repeatedly on the long drive to work. I am not sure this is what Louise Hay had in mind!

As the days and weeks went by I became more settled and convinced myself that life was great. But the cracks started to show. The more I hooked, the more I used, and I began to drink quite heavily. My long-lost lover reappeared in crystalline white powder form and flaunted her availability. One night Trixie with the Marilyn Monroe hair asked me if I wanted some shnarf. I discovered that shnarf or shnarfing was the colloquial name for cocaine, and apparently it was a much cooler term than 'blow' or 'snort'. Well, I had to agree that 'snort' was also an ugly word. I mean 'snorting cocaine' hardly sounded attractive. But to be honest, 'shnarfing coke' sounded even more revolting to me. Clearly I was no longer part of the fast and fabulous; this was 1993 and I had stopped indulging in nose candy back in 1981. In my day we had called it 'toot'. We'd thought it sounded really sophisticated to talk about 'tooting cocaine' or going off to buy toot.

So on this particular night I found myself shnarfing coke with Trixie and two 'steamers', the name we used to refer to clients. The brain never forgets, and as the cocaine did its thing, it was all so familiar and, within minutes, I felt great. Throwing any caution to the winds with abandon, I welcomed my mistress back with open arms, choosing to forget how she had previously brought me to my knees.

As Styx sang, I was 'tricked with visions of paradise'. In 1981, the album from Styx, Paradise Theatre, became my benchmark of coçaine chic, the song 'Snowblind' my signature tune. Today I can see how appropriate the lyrics were.

Coke was my nemesis. After that one night, I went straight back to using every day. A few weeks later I overheard one of my regulars say to his mate, 'Well, I was going to go with Paris, but she looked so drugged.' I heard it but blocked it out quickly and made it all about him. 'He was such an asshole anyway, etc., etc.' Within minutes, the comment was gone and I continued as before.

One day Larry asked me if I would go with one of his cop buddies. There were always cops coming in and out of The House – always being treated like royalty. My immediate response was, 'What if he doesn't like me?' One of the girls who had become a new friend, and Larry, came back almost in unison with, 'What's the problem? You've got a cunt, haven't you?' Lesson number 3; Men aren't fussy when it comes to sex. The rose-coloured spectacles were coming off.

My body also started displaying symptoms of my lifestyle. Incredibly, I contracted measles; a childhood illness and at my age wasn't much fun. Run down and fatigued, I was getting warning signs, but at that stage I was completely incapable of acknowledging, let alone interpreting distress.

Then Larry asked me to go with another cop and something inside me snapped, and I walked out. Up until then it had felt like I'd made my own choices regarding the men I had gone with, but now I felt exploited, and I had to leave. I remember Larry calling to me, 'You'll be back, Paris,' and as I headed for my car, I turned round and offered a weak 'Never' in rebuttal.

But this defection was not the victory it might have been, because I continued to endanger myself by 'working' from home for the next seven months.

# 10

## La Duchesse

And so I continued to ply my questionable trade from home. Although I'd managed to secure a few regulars who followed me from The House, I needed to find a more reliable source of referral. This is how I came to meet Gigi, a larger-than-life 'madam' who owned an up-market escort agency. Actually her business purported to be a reputable dating agency, but behind the genteel facade of respectability there existed a far more lucrative enterprise.

I had seen an ad under the social column headed 'Meet your Soulmate'. The ad seemed perfectly respectable but I sensed something a bit offbeat behind the scenes, so I called the number and went to meet Gigi at her home, from which she ran her business. She explained that men would pay a once-off fee to join her service, and agreed to send whoever she could my way. They would then pay me independently. This arrangement suited me perfectly.

Gigi was about forty kilograms overweight and, in my insecurity,

I loved this about her, because it made me feel thin and attractive by comparison. Our relationship was also helped by the fact that she too abused pharmaceuticals. Our partnership was more strategic than anything else – we were both most concerned about what we could get from each other. In truth she irritated me enormously. I couldn't see it then, but the reason she annoyed me so was because she mirrored my defences. Her over-the-top, fluorescent personality was more like my own than I cared to admit, and really just a mask for her insecurity.

At The House I had found a false sense of power in selling my body, but this bravado was starting to pall, and in addition to all the drugs I was taking, I was drinking more and more champagne in a vain attempt to manufacture sparkly feelings and make my clients feel comfortable. It's an interesting phenomenon that the men I saw felt a need to be liked and accepted by the person they were paying for sex. On the one hand, the anonymity of a paid-for encounter suited them, but on the other, the frailty of their egos meant that they wanted reassurance that this was more than a commercial transaction. For me, it was always about the money, in the sense that if I hadn't seen the client through a lens softened by whatever the agreed upon rate was, nothing could have induced me to perform the acts that I carried out. It wasn't about liking the person or not; it was more about the affirmation I got from the fact that someone was willing to pay to have sex with me. But it became hugely tedious when having to pander to clients' flimsy sense of selves; I came to realise that men who paid for sex were intrinsically insecure about who they were, both as men and as people.

One night I was booked for a threesome at the clients' apartment. Being without boundaries meant that over and above the inherent hazards of the work, I willingly endangered my life by going to strangers' homes alone. I never really knew exactly what or who I would be faced with. I rationalised this recklessness by soothing myself with glib statements like, 'It's okay, Gigi knows where you are, nothing will happen to you!'

I arrived at this couple's house in the middle of who knows where to discover that they had no booze. Despite being heavily 'medicated', I could not perform without the help of alcohol, so I made the husband go out and hunt down an open bottle store. While I waited for him to return, I had a fleeting moment of sanity as I reflected on how estranged from reality I had become. Unfortunately, this feeling was not to become an Aha moment, as he soon returned, armed with booze, and I proceeded to get completely trashed and do what it was I had been paid to do.

I was quite unresolved as to how I felt about women. For the past few years I had been involved in an extremely dysfunctional relationship with a woman called Shelley. I was attracted to women who had lots of male energy and she was quite masculine. She could also drink more than anyone I had ever met and was a maudlin drunk – which was most unattractive, but at the same time there was something appealing about her; perhaps it was her vulnerability. Shelley was volatile and high maintenance and ours was one of those on-off, destructive relationships characterised by monumental histrionics. To make matters more complicated, I was also seeing someone else at the same time.

In the late eighties, after leaving The Company, I spent a few years working at an academic bookshop. Grey was a student who worked there part time to earn extra money. He was also ten years younger than me. He was very good looking and well over six feet tall, with light, sandy-coloured hair and a soft crinkly smile. He had a great body from playing sports and working out in the gym. I couldn't believe he wanted to be with me, and yet he was besotted. It was fantastic! But once again, I couldn't do sex. I craved the intimacy, or so I thought, but at the same time it repelled me.

As we lived together I felt a certain degree of obligation to have sex, and hence every touch became associated with it. I found a number of ways to avoid having sex, not least of which was to leave the relationship. But then I'd miss him, thinking I had made a terrible mistake, and beg him to take me back. This pattern went on for a number of years. It was a seesaw of jangled nerves, sick pride and make-up sex (which, for some reason, I could do).

In between all of this I would run back to Shelley, who would tell me, 'But Joanne, you know you're gay.' And she'd say to Grey. 'Isn't it lucky that you two have broken up? After all, Jo's a dyke!' I would cringe inside because I didn't know what I was.

And then, in 1990, I met Leandre, or Lili, as I called her. Just to add fuel to the enormous fire that was my love life, I was convinced she was the one, and, on an impulse, asked her to move in with me after having known her for only a few days. It was all rather sweet and my family thought I'd 'finally found myself', except, once again, I couldn't really have sex with her. Nothing to do with her – she was gorgeous. She had short brown hair that was cut into the nape of her beautiful neck, enormous violet brown eyes and the naughtiest smile I had ever seen. We tried so hard. I remember how on New Year's Eve we drank a bottle of tequila and watched *Jean de Florette* and *Manon of the Spring*. It was intimate and romantic and we had sex, but it was stressful for me and I wished with all my heart that things could be different.

Although I was attracted to women on a certain level, I struggled to be intimate sexually. I liked the idea of being involved with women, but the reality proved to be too difficult. With men it's possible to lie back and 'think of England', so to speak, and get through the act, or even participate at some level, without feeling anything. With women it's different. With women I think one needs to be present and active, which I completely lacked the capacity to do then. I could engage sexually with women in my role as a 'working girl', because in that context I had nothing to prove and was able to dissociate. I was a good technician, so to speak, but it was completely meaningless, and that really was the point.

As I persisted in pushing my limits, I continued to disregard any sense of personal preservation, until one day I was involved in a motor accident that completely wiped out my car. Although I walked away unscathed, the accident was a wake-up call – of sorts.

That night was the opening of one of my client's new men's club, which I had agreed to run. Clearly the accident was a sign that this wasn't meant to be and so, even though I may have been able to work out lifts, I withdrew from that scheme and continued to sell my services from the relative safety of my home.

It was soon after the accident that I met Terry the Slave. Terry reminded me of a very tall imp with his rosebud lips and big ears. He had a wicked tongue and would keep me in fits of laughter, which I really enjoyed. Terry and I ended up on the same frequency because, as I was to discover during our first session, Terry did not want sex. Rather, he was into being a slave and actually wanted me to be his mistress. At first, rather naively, I had no idea what this meant. I learnt that it translated into him being willing to do absolutely anything for me. Terry's story was that he had been hideously abused by his mother for years, and even though he was married, the only relationship in which he felt truly comfortable was with a dominatrix. He was also eager to impart his knowledge about this murky world of domination, submission and bondage. Though this was not a world that resonated with me at all, it did seem like a profitable alternative to what I was doing and, most appealing of all, it meant I wouldn't have to have sex!

My transformation from Paris to La Duchesse began, and Terry proceeded to inundate me with reading material on S & M – magazines with weird and wondrous titles and even more bizarre content, which he had been subscribing to for years. He also helped me turn my bedroom into a veritable dungeon of delight, or horror, depending on your particular penchant. I had to persuade Grey, with whom I was still living, that transforming our sleeping space into a temple of doom was a good idea. I promised that I would uninstall everything by the time he came home and, amazingly, he agreed. He didn't ask questions, and I think he preferred to know as little as possible.

Wooden tawses, whips, chains, ropes and canes in various lengths and widths went up on the wall and Terry and I swapped my curtains for heavier ones so that it was dark at all times. I discovered that it was not as easy as one might have thought to go out and purchase things like canes. It wasn't as if I could announce to the shop assistant, 'Hi, I am looking for a couple of canes I can use to beat the shit out of my clients!'

At first there were no canes to be had in the whole of Johannesburg. Then Terry came across a factory quite far out town that sold a variety of canes in different lengths and widths. This was exciting. I could have a formidable collection! I set about choosing the ones I wanted, brandishing the different canes through the air like a demented person, until I realised that the sales assistant was staring at me open mouthed. I was so embarrassed that I wanted to run out of the shop, but Terry reminded me who I was and I calmed down. We bought the canes and I walked out of there like the Duchess I had become.

Soon, I had a fully kitted out dungeon including a medieval stocks and a rack (more for show than for actual use), which Terry made with his own hands. I concocted a suitable dominatrix outfit; a classic French designer dress, a keepsake from my gallery days, rounded off with the trashiest shoes that I ever had the misfortune of wearing – their perilously high heels gave me just the right cachet which, in my opinion, a dominatrix with style and presence needed. Next I began advertising under the sobriquet La Duchesse in *The Star*. Before long my services were in great demand and I had a steady string of regulars.

This new venture left me wide open to some deviant people, and given that I was not in the most stable period of my life, there seemed to be no way to shield myself from them. Hence I was forced to deal with some pathologies which left me quite deadened. For instance there were clients who wanted 'golden showers'. I had to have that one explained to me by Terry, 'Urinate over them, Madame.' 'Not in this lifetime!' was my response. Or worse, there were the ones who wanted me to defecate over them. Of course, or maybe not of course, given my own dysfunction, I could not and would not fulfil these and some of the sicker desires of my clients.

One of the problems I encountered was that my clients assumed I was equally aroused as they were by what I did, and just as twisted. This couldn't have been further from the truth. In reality, the whole thing repulsed me and there were moments when I regarded the clients as freaks. Although I knew that they were damaged, there was a part of me that felt disgusted by their vulnerability and neediness. I admit that watching them demean themselves made me feel well in comparison, but after the session I would feel sickened. Obviously it was not in my interest to disabuse them of their fantasies about me, but sometimes it became hard to keep up the pretence. I had this urge to scream out 'I'm not like you!' But I was. Perhaps my illness didn't manifest in the same way, but otherwise I was no different from or lesser than them, and deep down I knew it. I realise that it was my own condition that created the illusion of being superior, but I think I had to take this stance to be able to function.

Having listened to Terry's stories about his encounters with other doms where apparently anything went – from dangerous levels of physical abuse to acts involving excrement that I could never have imagined – I was determined to do things differently, sticking to far tamer punishments and refusing to do anything too bizarre or risky. My approach was more psychological and theatrical than painful or abusive. I was good at playing the role of intimidating authority figure, and for many of the men who came to me, this surrendering of authority was part of the appeal. They were often high-powered executives who were used to having to make decisions at all times, and when the roles were reversed this could be quite heady.

One such client was Mike, a wealthy and successful CEO of a large corporation. In his fifties, Mike had the appearance of a bullmastiff, complete with jowls and a hangdog expression. My sessions with him followed a set script. I would begin by ordering him to repeat the initials of La Duchesse while whipping him using an exquisite, soft brown leather riding crop. This crop was my trademark and I kept it with me at all times. Next I would manacle his arms and legs to the wall so that he was completely helpless and powerless.

'Mmm, Mikey, I'm wondering what I'm going to do with you today? Put you in the stocks or …' I would say, or words to that effect.

'Oh no Duchesse, please don't …" Mike might interject.

'Did I say you could interrupt me? Right, that's the stocks for you. Let's teach you some manners.'

Then I'd put him in the stocks and tell him, 'Now Mikey, I'm going out, I don't know when I'll be back, so be good and behave yourself.'

Telling clients that I was leaving usually gave them quite a fright as they had no way of knowing whether I was being serious or not.

The first time I did this to Mike I left the room for about fifteen minutes. By the time I came back, he was decidedly subdued. I undid his arms and legs and made him lie down on the carpet and tied him up with rope. Then I took some multicoloured clothes pegs and 'lovingly' rubbed them over his chest, and just as he was feeling complacent, I slammed them over and clamped them onto his nipples.

'That should be enough to get the adrenalin going,' I said.

He wriggled around, becoming quite aroused. I looked away.

'Who gave you permission to get an erection?' I asked in a thundering voice.

'No one,' said a very small voice.

'Exactly,' I said, 'so now you need to be punished. What do you think a suitable punishment might be?'

'A hundred lashings with the cane?' said he, ever hopeful.

'We'll make it five,' I sighed.

'Yes, La Duchesse.' He then entreated, 'Please, please, Madame La Duchesse, may I kiss your foot?'

'Hmph,' I snickered. 'What, an unworthy wretch like yourself? Why would I allow that?'

'Because I worship the ground you walk on,' he implored, and continued to beg for the honour of kissing my feet. Eventually I allowed him to kiss my shoe and he slobbered all over it in an effort to show his devotion. I then stood up and ground my stiletto heel into his nipple. He groaned with the mixture of pain and pleasure and I felt a mixture of revulsion on the one hand and pride on the other at being able to evoke such a response.

He was now ready to be caned. I chose the cane and began counting from five downward. Whoosh went the cane, slicing through the air and landing on his bottom. After this, the session was more or less over and the only thing that remained was for Mike to masturbate.

I, being Madame La Duchesse, never participated in this part of the session. The truth was I was still unable to touch a man's penis, so I managed to carry off a fairly flawless performance of being far too high and mighty to stoop to such levels, convincing my clients that they should be eternally grateful that I would even deign to be in the same room while they brought themselves to climax. It mostly worked; after all, this was not a shared exchange, and I was not open to negotiations. Most of my clients returned so I could only assume that I had carried it off. The irony of all of this was that the power really vested in the submissives who, after all, by electing to be in pain not only didn't have to deal with their issues but were actually more in control and ended up manipulating the doms. All the same, I was grateful to not be having sex and, if truth be told, thankful I didn't hurt anybody considering the state I was in.

Irrespective, it was disconcerting to witness just how much hurt or downright torture these men desired. There's a very thin line between so-called consensual sadomasochism and abuse for someone who ostensibly had no boundaries. I have no idea how I managed to set reasonable limits and maintain them. Perhaps I knew unconsciously that one day I would be able to use all these experiences to help guide my future therapy clients as they navigated the underworld of their own psyches. Notwithstanding my spiralling emotional state, I kept a fairly thorough file on each client that crossed my threshold; it made me feel that I was at least taking some steps for my safety as well as theirs. I half-jokingly called it my 'blackmail file', as some of my clients were well known in the community. What I couldn't have predicted was how useful and valuable all this sensitive information would be in the years ahead when I became a counsellor with a special interest in sexuality.

I've seen so many programmes over the years in which, for example, doms reveal that they feel S & M is a healthy way for men to express themselves. And invariably there are any number of psychologists who will agree. Based on my own experience, I disagree. I found that there was always something that could be traced back to childhood problems, and the client was merely repeating an embedded pattern or patterns. Even a small cruelty can be eroticised as sadism, as can any transgression of a boundary be sexualised as masochism. It's often not as simple as direct cause and effect, and while the client may find relief in the 'scene', there are other ways of coping that are possibly healthier if less instantly gratifying.

Terry was always around to help and support me, but as the weeks spun by I felt I was bleeding energy that I didn't really have. It was hard to listen to all the messages on my answering machine; some of them were from hard-core criminal types who clearly got off on scaring people like me. It worked, because I became fearful and began to see shadows in shadows. Once again I felt my life slip out of control. So I did what I always did in a time of crisis – I sliced my wrists and ended up in casualty.

The next day I landed up at Gigi's house. It was Christmas Eve and Gigi, who was now about thirty days clean, having recently been to rehab, was having an Oros party (I mean, really!) for all her clean and sober friends. And me. I was completely freaked out by this idea but nevertheless hung around. Off my head on all my pills I walked around holding my bottle of vodka as all these born-again Narcotics Anonymous people tried to tell me that I really needed help.

I lasted a few hours with these strangers until finally the comments and advice-giving became so unbearable that I decided the only solution was to off myself once and for all. This time I would make sure my methods were foolproof. I called a taxi to take me back to my place, before I could change my mind. As I waited outside for my ride, I thought about one of my favourite paintings, *The Two Fridas* by Frida Kahlo, a double self-portrait that she painted in 1939 at the time of her divorce from Diego Rivera. The traditional Frida is presented to us, the audience, with her shattered heart exposed, and a cut artery drips blood onto her dress. I felt that I could identify with her pain; here was someone who was wounded in body and in her heart. The other Frida is healthy, representing her stronger side. Frida's story had always struck a chord with me; like me, she was never at peace with the conventions of her time. I wondered momentarily if, like the alter egos in her painting, I too might have a strong side that could take over in times of adversity. But then my cab arrived and any thoughts of redemption were blown away as my thoughts became fixated on my imminent plans of destruction. Which is how, on the eve of Christmas 1993, I came to be sitting on a window ledge, weighing up the pros and cons of hurling myself off.

# 11

## Rehabilitation

'Jump – just do it,' exhorted one of the voices in my head, incitingly. 'Yeah, but what if the fourth floor isn't high enough?' Your luck, you'll end up a paraplegic!' taunted another, with a certain amount of schadenfreude.

I was sitting on the ledge of my windowsill with my legs dangling over the road below. Smoking one cigarette after another, I had created a dense, grey acrid cloud around me.

It was windy. I shivered. My arms were starting to ache. I looked down at the bandages; white and pristine, in stark contrast with the angry and jagged wounds they concealed. Suicide attempt number fifteen. If I jumped, this would be it; there would be no number sixteen.

Suddenly I felt myself being wrenched backwards and crash-landing unceremoniously onto the carpet in the room behind me. It felt like half my skin had been removed from my back and thighs. 'What the …!' It was Grey. Dear sweet Grey. Driving back to our apartment, he had seen me from his car, perched on the ledge, and like an Arthurian knight he'd charged upstairs to save me. Now, having been brought down to earth quite literally, and feeling unnaturally sober, I started to cry hysterically.

'Phone Dr Feelgood,' recommended Grey assertively. 'He's on holiday,' I replied in a barely audible voice between sobs, knowing somewhere within me that part of this acting out was my reaction to Dr Feelgood being away. 'But I could call his locum,' I offered up reluctantly, half-whispering the words. The truth was I'd rather have walked naked down the main road, but my back was against the wall. So I found the locum's number and made the call, shaking like a deranged tumble dryer. After several rings I got her on the other side of the phone and told her my sad little tale. First there was silence and then she replied in a completely flat, detached, 'I really couldn't care less' tone, 'There is nothing I can do for you. It's Christmas night.'

Beside myself with rage at her cavalier response, I shrieked and hurled abuse down the telephone. She was completely unmoved. I put the phone down and, feeling hopeless and shattered, suggested to Grey that perhaps I should call Riverfield Lodge, the rehabilitation centre where Gigi had gone. Thankfully, I got through to a sympathetic person. She listened to my crisis and then explained, 'Well, it certainly sounds like you really need to be here, but we cannot admit you tonight; it's Christmas night.' Briefly I wondered at the exigency of the professionals to keep Christmas sacrosanct from personal trauma. My heart tumbled, because for a few moments I had been feeling like there was a miniscule part of me that could, just maybe, fight this fight. So, very simply, I said, 'If you don't take me now I'm going to be dead by the morning.' She must have heard the sincerity in my voice, because somehow, thirty minutes later, I was on my way to Riverfield.

Within those thirty I managed to throw handfuls of pills down my throat in an effort to calm myself down, but also, who knew when I'd be able to use again? The irony of using copious amounts of drugs on my way into rehab clearly escaped me. Thankfully I didn't yet know the concept of 'total abstinence', as this would probably have been too much for me to handle.

It was a long drive to the centre. Sprawled out on the back seat, near catatonic, as much from the events of the night before as from the many substances I'd consumed, some of the beliefs and convictions I'd held for so long drifted into my mind. I'd always believed that I would die from either a drug overdose or from committing suicide, and was content with this. I'd also been convinced that I would die before the age of thirty. Thus I was confident that I would never have to face the consequences of my addictions and life choices, because I thought I would be dead before that happened. Well, I was thirty-eight years old, alive, if barely, and on my way into rehab, where anything could happen. And it seemed that a part of me, albeit a small part, was willing to choose life. Well, 'willing' may have been going a bit far – it wasn't as if I was brimming over with love and joy at the prospect of change. But even I could see that I had run out of all other options.

These thoughts were interrupted as suddenly the car screeched to a halt. Grey had missed the turning and had to turn around. Shocked out of my comatose state, I was suddenly frightened about what lay ahead. In some ways I had reason to fear; certainly, my life would never be the same again.

Staying in rehab was a bit like being in a time warp where time stood still. I wish that I could remember all the colourful characters that made up my inmates and fellow travellers, but most of my stay was seen through a hazy screen of detox medication, and only a few incidents stand out.

On my arrival my bags were dutifully searched and the nurse came out with a tray piled miles high with boxes and packets of pills, apparently all mine. I was quite shocked, as a big part of my denial meant that I never really knew just how much I was popping. The next morning I met the medical staff, who were made up, amongst others, of the very handsome Dr Caring, a recovering pethidine addict, and the equally gorgeous Dr Treasure, who was in recovery from self-harm. I was put onto detox meds and warned that the process was going to be tough. They told me that because I was such an incorrigible and relentless addict, who had been using for such a long period of time, the powers that be had decided they could not assign me to just any counsellor. If I was to have any chance whatsoever, I needed their heavyweight therapist, but he was only returning from leave within the next ten days. Instead of being daunted or depressed by this, the overdeveloped junkie pride in me was flattered, and I preened at being considered such a potentially formidable client.

In the meantime, I became acquainted with my fellow rehabees and, true to form, it was less than a day before I was drawn to a pretty face and blithely dove into a 'jailhouse romance' with someone as vacant and effete as myself. To my shame, I was soon prancing around hand in hand with Beau the space cadet, as though I hadn't a care in the world. Beau was a charmer, if rather soft and a bit of a chinless wonder. I think I was drawn to him as he was also a cocaine addict. It was a careless and dangerous distraction, and on about the second day of me behaving like a silly, infatuated teenager, one of my peers told me that Beau had been all loved up with another patient only days before my arrival. Given my predilection for looking for love in the wrong places, this information on its own was not enough to pry me away, especially since my mangled little brain had already been working overtime conjuring up Utopian images of happily ever after. But fortunately, over the next few days I managed to drift away from him almost organically; I'm sure that I used him as a temporary anaesthetic while reeling from the shock of coming to terms with being in rehab.

The programme itself was a bit of a hit and miss affair, and if I have to compare it to how I would come to know treatment in the following years, I would probably be quite critical. But in terms of offering me a safe space for twenty-eight days, I can never express my gratitude adequately. Ultimately, I am a prime example of my belief that when one becomes willing, it really doesn't matter where one is; recovery will happen when one is prepared to work at it, regardless of whether one is in a five-star treatment facility or in a more modest rehab, or even if one is not in treatment at all and finds recovery in other ways.

There was an incredibly competent occupational therapist there who, besides being possessed of an annoyingly cheerful disposition, put together these structured groups which focused, for example, on memory. 'Let's see how many brain cells these degenerate addicts have lost due to their drugging and/or drinking.' I couldn't tolerate these sessions. I felt like such a failure; other people seemed to be able to remember much more than me and, anyway, didn't I already know that my short-term memory was shot?

And then there was the withdrawal. Intense cramps and aches, constant nausea and sometime vomiting and retching, which for me was absolutely hideous. I may have suffered from various manifestations of eating disorder for years, but I could never have been a bulimic; I found the act of vomiting unbearable. Nothing could have prepared me for that; I felt l ike I was dying. And then two weeks later, when the benzo withdrawal really kicked in, I hoped I would die. It was completely savage and merciless. I didn't know what to do with myself. I couldn't sit, I couldn't lie down, I couldn't walk around, I was a catalogue of can't, couldn't and more couldn'ts. I felt so uncomfortable in my own skin, like I was in exile from my own body and was about to explode from the inside out, or was it from the outside in? I seemed to be deteriorating, so I was put back onto another brief course of detox meds and this time it was Physeptone, or Methadone, as it's more commonly known, and as I drank my final sip of the 'juice', almost licking the glass to make sure I got it all, I could feel every last drop drizzle into me, reaching every cell in my body and bringing a welcome respite from the creaking cramps in my joints and bones that I had come to believe would last forever. The headaches were relentless; it was just a question of degree. My group could tell what time it was from the black lines under my eyes, which became more deeply etched halfway down my face later on into the day. I was a complete mess, but somehow I was hanging in there. I didn't know how or why and I didn't need to, I just was. In the beginning I harassed the nursing staff for pain meds – back then detox regimes were fairly basic and strict and I was allowed a rather foul potion of Panado mashed into Brufen, which might have helped if the Brufen had not been so aggressive that it wiped out my stomach in a minute. So eventually I became quite stoical about what I was going through and stopped asking for the pain meds. In any case, it served mostly as a placebo. It was really the act of pill-taking that momentarily soothed me.

Ironically, considering the amount of toxins I was always willing to put into my system, I had become a fairly committed vegetarian over the past couple of years and as the centre's chef was away on holiday I was forced to subsist on toast and watermelon. I survived really well, as it happened, and became quite accepting of the inconveniences as I quickly realised that these were small things and I really was not there for the food. I would sit in group meetings and listen to my peers complain endlessly about all sorts of trivial matters in an effort to avoid themselves. I remember one day in group the leader announced, 'We have to talk about the coffee mugs!' There was an instant, collective sigh of displeasure. 'Oh for fuck sake,' said one of the inmates (that's what we called ourselves). 'Do we have to talk about the coffee mugs at every meeting?'

'Boring!' booed another.

'Well,' said the group leader, 'if everyone washed their mugs then we wouldn't be having this conversation.'

On and on they went, the voices growing more vociferous as people started pointing fingers. And we were no closer to a solution.

Over the years, in my work at other treatment centres, I came to see how this type of petty griping was a reliable indicator of the wellness of those participating. There will always be a coffee mug story just as there will always be a smoking in the toilet story; it was the intensity of the complaining that reflected where people are in their recovery.

Previously, I would probably have been group leader in these gripes, but this time, remarkably, something had started to shift. It was almost imperceptible at first, but then I met the Brahman of addiction therapy at the time, The Man, my hero not only of the hour but of the next few years, as he successfully facilitated and supported me through my life with the commitment and skill of the gifted healer that he truly was and I am sure still is. The Man wasn't a hunk in the traditional sense, but he was attractive in a rugged way. He looked exactly like I thought a male therapist should, right down to the corduroy trousers and beard, which he seemed to wear longer or shorter depending on his mood. His hair was long and sometimes tied back in a ponytail, and he had beautiful green eyes behind sexy, intellectual specs. He wore cardigans at a time when I don't think many men wore them and for me this was a sign that he was okay with himself. And that was important for me. With his help, I overthrew my archaic system and started to restructure and reformat. Like with any coup, I would experience great resistance, and one of my biggest challenges would be to learn to find a way to access those parts of me that feared change.

I remember that in my first interview with him I threw out a challenge, 'Well, I must warn you that I've been able to manipulate every therapist I've ever seen.' Behind my clumsy revelation I was really asking, or perhaps pleading, to know if he would be the one who could contain me. I can't remember his exact response, but unlike most of the other professionals I had consulted over the years, he didn't rise to my bait. He simply supported me where I was in the moment. I felt quite exhilarated, and it proved to be an important starting point from which the Lego-block process of building trust could grow.

My family reserved judgement about my latest hospitalisation. I had once been to the Morningside Clinic and stayed in a luxury ward to try to get off Stopayne. I was put onto all sorts of drips, and experienced no discomfort at all. It was fabulous. When I got out, it was simply a matter of time before I started using again. So this time they weren't holding their breath. They had heard my protestations of 'I'll never use again' or 'I'm finished with this rubbish' or 'I promise I'll never cut myself again'. In fact they were so sceptical this time that they were unwilling to help financially. Grey paid, for which I am forever indebted.

I did feel a bit punished by their lack of support. Nobody came to visit me and only my mother stayed in touch with me. And this was probably more that I stayed in touch with her. But considering what I'd put them through, who could blame them? Of course, back then, as much as I tried, I didn't yet have the capacity to really understand what I had done to them, because as much as I was changing in leaps and bounds, it was still all about me. I would truly see how much I had hurt them only much later, through the ashen, ravaged faces of the families of the clients that I would work with. Only then could I really assimilate, on an emotional level, the hell-ride that I had dragged my family through for as long as I could remember.

In my opinion, I was too sick physically to properly engage in all the group activities at the centre. Although I probably could have been nudged into participating more, happily for me, nothing was compulsory. This allowed me to pick and choose in terms of what could only loosely be called a programme, which suited me fine, particularly as there was a certain therapist that I was studiously avoiding as far as possible. I was completely repelled by Dr Phoney, the suave and impeccably dressed clinical psychologist who managed to push such a massive button in me. He managed to make me feel like Jo Jo the fatty all over again, clumsy and inadequate. It was painful. He was young and arrogant, but despite his youth he reminded me of my father. So in spite of my dislike of the man, I unconsciously set myself up by looking for some kind of affirmation from him which clearly I was never going to get. I could feel and sense his judgement of me energetically, but then I would start to doubt my own reality and think, Maybe he isn't judging, how could he be judging? After all, he was the professional and I the mere patient. If I was a bit uninspired about the groups, I felt the exact opposite about my one-on-one time with The Man, which I wouldn't have missed for anything, including being headached from hell. My time with him was my first experience of a sacred space, and I cherish those hours to this day. I believe that I went to Riverfield at least in part to meet The Man, who was about to resign and go into private practice. It seemed to all happen at exactly the right time.

One afternoon we were treated to an educational video on family dynamics, and as I watched my entire life unfold before my eyes on the screen, I became quite animated and couldn't wait to let my mother know of my latest revelation. Not the most brilliant idea I had ever come up with. As I enthusiastically regaled my mother with 'Ma, I learnt today that we are probably the most dysfunctional family on the planet,' there was a deathly silence, and my long-suffering mother was probably wondering where and when it was all going to end.

At one particularly low point I remember crying to Dr Caring, desperately worried that I wasn't going to make it, and he turned around to me and very quietly but firmly said, 'Joanne, you need to start praying.' At first I became prickly, defensive, infuriated, and retorted, 'You don't even know me, how is praying going to help my situation?' as I charged up onto my high horse. My experience with anything remotely spiritual up until then had not been all that positive. I had come from a middle-class Jewish family and up until the age of sixteen had been coerced into attending synagogue, after which I had dropped out. Without really knowing much about Judaism, I had dismissed it out of hand as being patriarchal, anti-feminine and irrelevant. Similarly, I saw God as this vengeful, punitive old man just waiting to strike me down. As I was about to flounce out of Dr Caring's office, I managed to pause and thought, 'Maybe I could try, what have I got to lose that I haven't already lost?' After all I'd lost absolutely everything – my son, my dignity, self-respect, values. The list was endless. So I might as well try praying. I went to my bedroom and knelt tentatively next to my bed, unsure what to do next. 'What would people think if they saw me like this? What would God think?' Then I got down on my hands and knees and started a dialogue with a power greater than myself. It was short and sweet, but it was something, and almost immediately miracles started happening. Now I am not referring to Angels coming down from Heaven, although I am definitely not excluding those, but what did happen was a change in perception; and the capacity to see things differently and not take things personally continues to be one of the cornerstones of my recovery process.

Looking back, what was so amazing is that I seemed to do so little; my Higher Power did the rest. In the beginning I couldn't 'do God', but the concept of 'the universe' worked for me. And then about a year later I heard myself talking about God. I have no idea when my Higher Power became God. I simply needed to pitch up for the recovery process and allow it and God to work in my life. And in one way or another, that is what I have been doing ever since.

At some point, another girl inmate arrived who made my own self-harm look like play-play tattoos. She had burnt her arms and legs beyond anything I thought possible and had caused some irreversible nerve damage. She was only twenty-two and had a family from nightmare-land which again made mine look like happy families by comparison. But pain is pain, and I distanced myself from her almost instinctively as she mirrored my own wounds so graphically and in my face. Evidently my attitude was all too obvious, and The Man bullied me into going to talk to her, assuring me that I would be able to assist her. I was mystified by this and quite petrified, as not only did I have no idea how to engage with people, but she hid behind a defensive umbrella of hostility. But I needn't have worried. When I plucked up the courage to approach her, my lacerated, scarred arms gave me credibility and gained me enough brownie points to be around her. Initially we just sat, holding space, and I guess it was my first encounter ever of a moment of empathy for someone else. It was a powerful connection, and though I really didn't have much to give, I could simply support and validate her through my own experiences. Once again, The Man knew what he was doing, and I was grateful for and enriched by this experience.

Toward the end of my stay I was allowed out for the weekend. To my surprise I couldn't wait to get back to the centre! Was I becoming institutionalised in such a short time? I suppose I wasn't ready yet. That weekend I had felt so unsafe out there in the real world, completely naked and exposed all the time. It was exhausting and enervating and as much as Grey tried to be solicitous, I couldn't or perhaps wouldn't talk to him. I felt so distant from him. This was the beginning of the end of our relationship.

One morning there was a bit of a scene going on, and I discovered that one of my inmates had managed to smuggle drugs onto the premises the previous evening and had used with a few other rehabees. My reaction completely floored me. I was visibly reduced to jelly and became angry with what I suppose was the inflated self-righteousness of the newly converted. But it went deeper then that. For the first time since being in treatment, I realised how easy it would have been to use, and, in a puff, all that I was trying to do would have instantly disappeared. It terrified me and I was thankful to still be in the centre to be able to process my fears. I realised that while there was a part of me that really wanted to be out of it and trashed so that I didn't have to deal with anything, I didn't want to go back to addiction. So I made a choice not to pick up. It was the first time I had taken responsibility for anything in a long time and it felt empowering. And although I hadn't yet been introduced to the twelve-step programme, I would discover that I had taken an important step in the right direction.

The days flew by and all of a sudden I had completed my four weeks. The counselling team were hugely negative about my prognosis and gave me no chance at all. According to them I was 'unrehabilatable'. Despite my progress, they simply couldn't move on from my original hardcore drug use. I was ambivalent about this feedback, and if part of it was supposed to scare me, it certainly added to my pre-existing fear of leaving what had become a sanctuary of sorts. I was apprehensive but my fear would keep me grounded. And I was also aware that as The Man was away at the time, this judgement came from people who really did not know me.

As I reluctantly took my first baby steps back into the real world I made another decision; I would do whatever it took not to end up back where I had come from, or dead. I didn't yet understand what that meant, but I knew that it came from a very deep, connected place within me, and that was enough.

# 12

## Recovery

For the first few months of recovery, I felt like a body of exposed nerves, constantly being triggered by everyday events. I didn't how to act. I didn't know how to be. After all, who was I without the use of pharmaceuticals or any of my other predilections? I didn't even know how to talk on the telephone! Everything seemed so strident and booming and quite overwhelming. I seemed to be experiencing life instantaneously, without any filters, and I didn't know what to do with this unexpected vitality.

Instinctively, I knew that all my previous coping mechanisms could take me back to using, so almost overnight I shut them down. I said goodbye to my razor blades, stopped acting out sexually and even refrained from seeking affirmation from men. As my body was craving sweet things, I abandoned my previous regime of prohibition and self-deprivation, giving myself permission to eat and stop worrying about my body image until further notice. I also realised that if I didn't devote myself to recovery and take it seriously, then I probably wouldn't stay clean.

With this in mind, I found my way to my first twelve-step Narcotics Anonymous meeting, which was held at the rather ghastly and dismal Yeoville Recreation Centre. At my first meeting, I sat in the closed circle and, despite my good intentions, found myself gazing around at this motley gathering of people and thinking, 'I'm not like them. What a bunch of losers!' Which was rich coming from me. I initially thought I'd wandered into a twelve-step Moonie sect, but quickly realised that although the members sounded a bit brainwashed, NA itself was far too disorganised to be a cult. There were people from all walks of life, from hardcore addicts who had lost everything to small-time users who were there to see if they had a problem. It was like one big dysfunctional family, so I felt right at home.

In spite of my initial resistance, I could feel an extraordinary energy at the meeting, which I would later define as 'Higher Power' stuff, and to which I was drawn. As I sat there I feigned indifference and inwardly scoffed at these people, but before the meeting's close I had come to realise that they at least knew how to stay clean for longer than five minutes. They also knew how to laugh at themselves. They were not particularly friendly towards me that first meeting, but they had something that I wanted. Sobriety. So I stayed. Besides, there was nowhere else to go; I had exhausted all other options.

Thus began my relationship with NA, which was certainly the place where I learnt the most about myself, often as reflected through other people. For instance I would sometimes become incredibly judgemental about somebody until eventually I would see that I was feeling condemnatory because there was some aspect of the person which reminded me of my own defences of character, either in the here and now or in the past.

Another thing I learnt was that secrets would keep me sick – I kept hearing about the importance of honesty. So in the spirit of forthrightness, one night I blurted out my sordid past. It was much more detailed than the average share in that in contained quite explicit content in terms of my prostitution. Disrespecting my right to anonymity, one of the 'old-timers' then proceeded to inform everyone who hadn't been at the meeting that night, and anyone new coming into the fellowship, about the contents of my share. I was really hurt and upset. As I was only six months clean when this happened, my first instincts were to blame him for my feelings, and in my resentment I almost missed out on a golden opportunity for growth. What I learnt from this experience was the difference between rigorous honesty and compulsive disclosure, and while it was a painful lesson to learn, I became more discerning over time. It was easy to be philosophical when my buttons weren't being pushed, but it was when I listened to hurtful gossip about myself that I made my more significant breakthroughs. The experience also taught me that what other people think or say about me is none of my business. Of course, keeping this truth in mind when people said hurtful things about me was easier said than done, especially with my tendency to take everything personally, but I found that I got better at getting over things more quickly the longer I stayed in recovery. A few weeks after getting out of rehab I went to see Dr Feelgood. Maybe I was hoping for and needing his approval, but what I received instead was, 'Joanne, you don't need to be so extreme – maybe some tranquilisers?' I ran away and never looked back. This proved to be a life-saving event, because after twenty-five years of relying on sleeping potions, my body was completely refusing or perhaps had forgotten how to nod off naturally. Who knows what I might have done in a weak moment during yet another night of counting sheep if I'd had easy access to drugs?

This sleeplessness went on for months. Night after night I would lie awake staring square-eyed at late-night TV, which then consisted of either CNN or Sky News. I spent many hours repeating what had become my mantra, the Serenity Prayer – 'God grant me the serenity to accept the things I cannot change; The courage to change the things I can; And the wisdom to know the difference' – and also the axiom 'This too shall pass', over and over until amazingly, at the point where the walls were starting to move and close in on me, I began to doze a few hours here and there. As Dr Caring had unsympathetically pointed out to me a few months previously, 'This is a consequence of your using! And you will not die from lack of sleep.' Nine months past, and just when I had started to believe that I would never know what it was to sleep through a night, I had my first full night's sleep. What a time for celebration! This was no small thing, believe me; it felt very precious.

In the last eight or so years of addiction, I used to have this window period of about half an hour in the morning when I'd taken all my pills and I'd briefly feel 'normal', like all was well in my world. During that time, I would ensure that I spoke to whoever I needed to, for example my mother, because after that it was downhill all the way. I would spend the rest of the day swallowing pill after pill in an attempt to regain that feeling of normalcy and at the same time to stave off withdrawal. Now the whole day stretched out before me and it was still quite a novelty that I wasn't dependent on any substance to determine its outcome. I found that I rose early and became a morning person. This from a former night owl who could barely tolerate the light of day. To this day I get up early, regardless of what I'm doing, otherwise I feel like I'm a using addict again.

I was quite lucky and blessed in that Perry, one of my cousins to whom I was quite close, had cleaned up in America from heroin at about the same time as me and returned to Johannesburg. We went through early recovery together and, aside from my cravings in those early months, we actually had fun. Perry was larger than life and also had a serious sex addiction. His girlfriend, Lucie, was a model and quite simply exquisite. I was in total awe of this Venus de Milo with her tawny complexion and reddish hair that fell halfway down her back. We went for coffees regularly and Perry and I attended NA meetings as often as we could. There were only three a week back then compared to over thirty a week now.

The twelve-step fellowship played a very important part in my recovery process, but I couldn't have done without the one-on-one therapy. Neither one was a substitute for the other. Some addicts find all their fulfilment in the twelve steps; for me they were a very important foundation; NA offered freedom from active addiction. But I needed to do a great deal more to take care of myself and to find the answers that would keep me clean.

By early 1994 The Man had opened his private practice and I started to see him one morning a week in addition to my thrice-weekly meetings. When I wasn't in meetings or therapy I spent my time seeing Perry and Lucie or devouring recovery books. Even though my concentration still wasn't fantastic and I sometimes had to read a page four times, it didn't matter. I couldn't get enough into my head. Of course, it was getting these messages into my heart that would be the real challenge. Slowly but surely the dense layers within layers of denial yielded to the persistent yet gentle challenges from The Man, and I began to face and examine the real Joanne. The Man also played a heroic role in helping me get beyond my somewhat rudimentary way of seeing things; I still regarded myself as the archetypal fuck-up and everyone else as perfect. He helped raise my consciousness to another level for which I am forever blessed.

Looking back, I think that my time with The Man was about acknowledging and owning those parts of me that I found quite loathsome, for example my feelings of shame and guilt and worthlessness, which were all-consuming. All of this had to be assimilated into consciousness before any transformation could occur. It took me a really long time to explore my shadow side, and there was work that I was unequivocally not ready to do. For example, I knew that my mother, who had always found any kind of sexuality distasteful, found me to be dirty in some way, and had called me a whore long before the word had become reality. I could acknowledge this but could not explore or investigate it further – it would have to wait until later; right then it was too painful. I think what was important was that I was putting in the hours of slog work so that it would be possible in the years to come to go deeper. At times, when memories grew too painful, I would shut down and retreat into a protective state. But there were moments when I would get in touch with something inexplicable. I would feel that being alive was fabulous and I would notice how exquisite everything was. It was these moments that I would try to drink in and imprint on my being so that I would remember the beauty when new difficulties arose.

As I approached the nine-month landmark, recovery started to remind me of labour; it was bloody, uncivilised and hugely painful. I remembered how, after being in labour for seventeen hours with Darren, I turned around to one of the sisters and said, 'Okay I've had enough now, I've changed my mind. I don't want this baby anymore, it's too sore!' After nine months of being clean, I was feeling the same way. I'd had enough! But of course, like after giving birth, I was yet to appreciate the full miracle of what had transpired.

And then one day I was a year clean, and though I wouldn't have said that I was happy – what was happy? – I was so grateful to be where I was and indeed to be alive! I could finally see that it really had been worth it. I was so proud of myself – it felt like the greatest achievement of my life and I was on a high. But then after a few days of triumph, the postpartum blues set in and I was left thinking, 'What now?' The doubt and anxiety didn't last long, thankfully, and I settled in to the new year with renewed hope and faith. This ceremonial ritual would play itself out every year at around the time it came closer to another year clean, and I would need to start ruminating about what the previous twelve months had been about.

Although the road to recovery had been quite agonising at times, it was always less chaotic than in the past. My mother died from a heart attack at around this landmark and although we never really talked about the past or became close, I like to think that at least she knew that I was getting better now and therefore she could leave. I know that she was proud of me; she simply lacked the capacity to express it. I struggled with my feelings when she died. I seemed to shut down my grief, but I also experienced a sense of relief, for her sake – she had developed emphysema, which had started to affect the quality of her life. This way, she went peacefully, without months or years of suffering indignities and ultimately a horribly painful death. These days I miss her a lot and I find myself talking to her. It's funny that way.

And then the miracles of recovery abounded as Darren came to live with me and I became a fulltime mother again for the first time in years. One day in early 1995 he simply arrived on my doorstep, having run away from home. And even though I had de facto custody and even though he was at an age where he could make up his own mind, I went to court to win back custody and I did. Both Darren and I were ecstatically happy, and as difficult as the court case had been, I felt that gaining custody was a huge step in terms of my being there for him. Years too late, perhaps, but it was a start.

Having Darren back in my life, for the first time I experienced happiness firsthand. This was a happiness unfiltered through any powdered lens, and I was so aware that this could never have occurred if I had still been using. I was also aware that I could never make up for a lifetime of being unavailable, and I needed to be present to his needs going forward one day at a time. It was as difficult for him as for me but somehow we navigated the journey.

Darren was always very protective of me, having been forced to play the caretaker role since a little boy, so if something happened in his life that he thought might upset me, he wouldn't necessarily tell me. He carried a lot on his shoulders. It would take some years to get through this. I am sure that I could write a book about the things that I did wrong in that time, but I know that I learnt to love unconditionally, and learning to become honest with each other has formed the framework of our very special bond ever since.

That time stands out as being incredibly special. I would go and watch Darren play rugby and occasionally embarrass him from the sidelines as I worried about him getting injured. He was a beautiful player and I loved it. I know he appreciated my being there and I don't think I missed a single game in those last two years of school. Having missed out on all his early school years, those rosy times are forever etched into my brain.

Within about ten months of being clean, another woman and I managed to start up the much needed and first Sex and Love Addictions Anonymous (SLAA) meeting in South Africa. Three or four of us came together once a week for a year and shared our dark stuff with like-minded people in our desperate desire to get well. That time was truly a turning point as I navigated my way through my prostitution days and spoke about my shame to people who didn't judge me. I moved ahead in leaps and bounds and thought that I was cured! But the universe was about to bring me down to earth in a big way.

When I was just over two years clean I met a drop-dead gorgeous man who was nine years younger than me and who, surprisingly but undeniably, showed an interest in me. My thoughts were, 'I'm so ready for this, this relationship is going to be perfect!' These days I'm able to have some compassion for my naivety. The Prince was also a crack addict, and back then I didn't understand why he would tell me that he was going to buy a sandwich and then disappear for two days. It was outside my experience, but I learnt quickly as he battled his demons, although he did have considerable clean time within our relationship.

Our intimacy brought out the parts of me that I struggled to acknowledge let alone work with. Jealousy, for example. I was so possessive that I felt toxic with resentment every time he so much as spoke to another girl. I couldn't believe that we were together and I felt threatened by the fact that his energies were so all over the place. Even though we were in a committed union, it was as though he wore an invisible label that said 'I'm available'. He was a great flirt and the women practically fell at his feet. He was like a younger version of me in addiction and, similarly, he used his looks and sex appeal as his personal measure of self-esteem. I felt diminished when I saw how he was looking at or talking to other women. The old voices in my head came back to taunt me, 'If only you were prettier, younger, thinner …' reawakening feelings of 'not being enough'. My insecurity came out as attempts to control and of neediness. And, to be brutally honest, it suited me for him to stay sick, because this meant that he continued to depend on me.

On the positive side, the relationship allowed me to reclaim my wounded sexuality, even if it was at a most elementary level. At the age of forty, scared and vulnerable, I had my first experience of clean and sober sex. He was everything that I could have wanted a lover to be – tender, gentle and exciting at the same time. There were moments when I really felt beautiful, and being with him helped me in my quest to love myself. This alone made my relationship with The Prince worthwhile.

When I finally had to leave the relationship because of my own addictive, co-dependent nature, I was completely devastated. I struggled to completely cut ties as I had made The Prince my new drug of choice, and there were times when I sat with my cellphone desperately daring myself to call but knowing that I would only make things worse. It was at this stage that the concept of 'one day at a time' really worked for me; sometimes it was as critical as, 'I won't call for the next five minutes.' It was frightening how deeply embedded my obsessive patterns still were, even after three years of being clean and having worked extensively on myself. But then at the same time, the roots of my co-dependency were emerging in therapy, so it was understandable that this behaviour was being triggered. I have discovered that whenever I am working on an issue, whether in therapy or on my own, I seem to attract similar situations into my life. My belief is that the universe gives me these opportunities to work through my stuff and to facilitate the healing process. I don't always get it right. And that is okay. It's about continuing on the journey.

Sadly I had no time to feel relieved at being out of the relationship as I was completely swamped by the intensity of the other emotions that were revealing themselves through therapy. It was then that I entered my first grieving stage since quitting my various addictions. I couldn't yet define or distinguish all the nuances of my grief. Everything I had been through was still too raw and unsophisticated, but I knew enough to know that it wasn't only about The Prince. I was lamenting other losses, including the ending of the relationship with Bared, which I had never even really acknowledged. Waves of anger and sadness washed over me as I felt emotionally connected to my experiences, and it really ached in places that I didn't even know could hurt. The Man was hugely supportive during this time but he also thought it a time for celebration, as I was finally feeling emotions I hadn't felt in decades. He couldn't contain his excitement and was just about doing a victory dance. I half wanted to kill him! He used to stand behind me sometimes in a session and put his hands on my shoulders and push down really hard, exerting a lot of pressure, hoping to induce a reaction, but I had felt nothing. I wasn't really in my body and it frustrated him enormously. My belief was that I had suppressed my feelings for over twenty-five years so they were not simply going to present themselves on demand now that I was clean. It was probably the most difficult time I went through in recovery.

I remember one session when The Man asked me quite gently, 'Jo, who does The Prince remind you of?' I sat back and thought about it and rather reluctantly had to come up with 'my father'. 'Good,' said The Man. 'And who else?' I racked my brains and eventually offered up a very weak 'Bared?'. It occurred to me that there were similarities between these three men, and even though they seemed so different, The Prince was really just another version of Bared, just less sophisticated and slicker.

I also started to experience feelings of rage around this time. I didn't know that I could feel that amount of emotion. But like some of my other issues, it was not the time to deal with it. Anger needs to be felt for some time, and goes through various stages, almost like an alchemical process, before it is turned into something meaningful. All I knew then was that acting on my anger was not very helpful, so I allowed myself just to feel it, which was transformative in and of itself. Dealing with it would be another story!

Another new feeling I experienced was what I called my 'abandonment' feeling. I would feel it physically as an ache just above my heart, and it would be breathtakingly painful for a moment, but then it would be gone. At the other end of the spectrum, I uncovered feelings of enoughness. I discovered that I was okay, and though it would probably take a lifetime to truly accept this, I was 'faking it till I made it', and it was working!

I was also going through a transformation from girl-woman to a mature woman, and for the very first time in my life, I felt an ancient, sacred connection to women everywhere. My life was no longer all about me, and when I sat in an NA meeting and heard women share their stories I felt a deep bond with them. I was definitely growing up. After my break up with The Prince, I quite recklessly agreed to a one-night stand with someone who was in a similar position to me in that he had recently broken up with his girlfriend. I found myself calling on the prowess of Paris to perform, as Joanne could not be present in such a premeditated but emotionless act. Even though I had been a willing partner, I felt like a prostitute, used and discarded, and for a while after that night it was easier to become a victim again and blame him for these feelings. However, I came to realise that my feelings of failure and rejection had nothing to do with him. The other incredibly important lesson I learnt from this one-night stand was that it was no longer an option for me to have casual or so-called recreational sex.

Although the experience almost threatened my sobriety, as it brought up huge feelings of shame, once again I was able to use the experience as an opportunity to claim some personal power. And it felt good. However, I didn't want to remember that night as my last sexual encounter, so I impulsively and quite injudiciously went rushing back for one final, lingering time in the arms of The Prince. And then I took a decision to become consciously celibate. There were many people who didn't understand and questioned my motives, but I felt happy and alive, and I kept to my resolution for many years. While I may not have been having sex or acting out sexually in any way, I believe that I still accessed my sexual energy as part of my overall creativity in terms of the passion that I showed in other areas of my life; it was around this time that I became involved in counselling, and my life became committed to helping facilitate the journey of others.

# 13

## Counselling

During my fourth year of recovery I was invited to become a trainee counsellor at a leading addictions centre in Johannesburg – I had been put forward by The Man, who was consulting at the centre. I was beyond speech with excitement and gratitude; once again I was conscious of the wonders of recovery, which allowed for such possibilities.

Soon after I started there, I was sent on an intensive group-therapy training course, in which one of the facilitators was The Man. It was experiential in that we, the staff members, were required to be group members for the duration of the course. Most of us didn't know each other very well, apart from two members who were friendly outside of the group. They would sit together and interact with one another to the exclusion of the rest of us, until, after one coffee break, The Man took it upon himself to split them up and asked Miss Mascara to move seats. Pink Shirt said nothing about this separation, and remained incredibly polite and courteous towards The Man. Barring his tight lips, one might have thought he was unaffected. In truth he was quite put out, which became apparent in his attention-seeking, passive-aggressive behaviour, directed at the co-facilitator, a woman. As the facilitators later explained to us in our debriefing, Pink Shirt was actually furious, but it was far too threatening for him to confront a man, and so he took out his frustration on a woman instead.

I had one Aha moment after another as these various processes were explained and experienced. I was captivated from the start by the organic nature of a group, where it's really difficult to manipulate the process. I could come in with an agenda but if the group was on another mission, it could spit me out, so to speak. Over the years I learnt to be big enough to honour the group's needs above my own and allow it to do what it needed to do without my own stuff getting in the way. For instance, group members could be talking about their mothers and I, as group facilitator, might have a need to know something about their fathers. I could interject, 'So I'm wondering where that left your fathers?' and if the group was on a roll talking about mothers, it could ignore my question completely. And that was okay. After all, it was about the good of the group.

The years that I spent at the centre were some of my happiest as I put in the hours and continued to develop my counselling skills. As a practitioner in training, group became my therapy of choice, and the one in which I had the most success. But I still had much to learn. In my early days, I inhabited a world of black and white when it came to recovery. I believed there was only one road to sobriety and wasn't willing to entertain any alternatives. In my view you were either using or not using, drinking or not drinking, and I could not understand or tolerate people who might be taking a small step forward by cutting down, for example.

This rigid stance impacted my work, and I quickly became renowned as 'the counsellor you love to hate'. My reputation preceded me to the point that new clients coming into the facility were scared to meet me. Far from being offended by this, I loved my new status. I remember telling a fellow counsellor that I was using 'La Duchesse energy'. I discovered that I only wanted to wear boots, summer and winter, with very tall heels, the higher the better. I would march down the passage, smiling to myself and conscious that everyone could hear the tap of my heels, which I felt added to my image as imposing authoritarian. When one of the client's wrote in his compulsory daily journal, 'Who the hell does she think she is? She is the Queen of Recovery and her heart is colder than my feet in winter,' instead of being upset, I was thrilled. His words reaffirmed my standing as the Ice Queen. I believed it was healthy for the clients to have to be respectful of someone. Of course, I tempered my strictness with a great deal of love and support, and by the time they left treatment, my clients usually had an enormous affection for me.

Interestingly, a number of people that I counselled in those years are still clean today and doing brilliantly, but I can definitely see the effect of my polarities on their perception of the world. They still have an attitude of 'It's my way or the highway'.

I adopted a distinctive hairstyle to match my new image; short at the back and sides, and with a very long fringe. Within that boundary I experimented with and interpreted 'my look', and having always had a penchant for hair colour, I went wild. Some months I would have blue and silver streaks, others purple and pink rounded off with gold iridescent sparkles. I adored constantly reinventing myself, and my early to late forties were a time of creativity and glamour. As I pursued my peacock range of hues, I would proclaim from time to time; 'Did I ever say that I wanted to look natural?' I suppose I was a bit outrageous, and fortunately my work environment was quite forgiving. I would tell my colleagues and clients that I was going to end up an eccentric old lady with a parrot, and that I was okay with this.

Everyone knew about Mignon the bird. I acquired her when I was a year clean. More human than parrot, she could swear like a sailor and had a wicked bite when she felt neglected. But to me she was an angel in parrot form (though I think she saw herself as more of an eagle), and from the first day, she became my constant companion. Only Mignon could drag me away from work. If she was sick and needed to go to the vet, I would drop everything to be with her. In later years, she was seen by the doyenne of animal healers, Daneen, whom I had met through a metaphysical counsellor friend, and on her recommendation, Mignon was trained to give Reiki healing through her wings. She still does. When I share this information with people, and I generally do not, their eyes glaze over and I am sure they think that I need to be certified while the music of the Twilight Zone plays in their head!

At the centre, I began to pay more attention to my food and body issues, which had been bothering me for a while but which I had put on the backburner while concentrating on getting clean. When it came to my body, I was still plagued by feelings of inadequacy and self-loathing. It was painful and difficult to love myself exactly the way I was. The more I tried the love thing, the more all the feelings of guilt and shame came up. I had to remind myself constantly that as powerful as they were, these feelings did not define me. I prayed hard, meditated often, and even if my capacity to quieten my mind lasted only minutes at a time, it all helped, and eventually I reached a point where I was able to say 'I, Joanne, love and accept my body in the here and now' and mostly mean it. Saying these words for the first time was a quite a victory, and in that moment of grounded spirituality, I made an important decision. I would never again deprive myself of any food. I had noticed how much of life I withheld from myself generally, and realised that food and the pleasure it offered was yet another of those things that I used to keep myself imprisoned. Making this decision felt self-loving and reflected the new me going forward.

I believe Overeaters Anonymous is great and works for many people, but I needed something different. While I understood abstinence around sex, I didn't, for example, want to never be able to taste sugar again. I had reached a stage where food represented a joyful celebration of life and I wanted to be part of all of it, within obvious boundaries like my vegetarianism. All my life I had feared food; it had been the enemy, yet it had preoccupied me every minute of the day. It made no difference whether I was in an abstinent, fasting phase, a binge mode or a so-called normal stage; food had been on my brain 24/7.

Simultaneous to my burgeoning self-acceptance, I started to experience what I had already known intellectually for some years; it's not what I eat that puts on the weight, it's how I think about what I eat that clutches the kilos. The guilt and the shame. This realisation was very exciting and though not always the easiest way to follow, it remains my philosophy.

I did have a wobbly around my body issue some years into recovery. I was due to meet my work colleagues at an art exhibition where a fellow counsellor, who was also an artist extraordinaire, was exhibiting his latest work. I went to change into an outfit that I had already selected, but as I looked in the mirror, I saw a whale reflected back to me, and I knew that all was lost. I tried on one thing after another, but to no avail. I could only see the whale. Don't get me wrong; I love whales, just not when they are being mirrored back at me! No matter how I tried to talk to myself, my powers of persuasion were completely unable to make the slightest dent in this powerful illusion of Joanne the Whale. I was crippled by my thoughts and feelings and ultimately unable to leave my townhouse. I called my colleague and mumbled my apologies with some excuse that sounded pathetic even to my ears. I did the same with my other peers, as there was no way that I could tell them the truth. Thankfully that was the last such experience to date.

I continued to excavate my life with The Man, who by then was also my peer. I was thrilled when he invited me to co-facilitate an after-care therapy group, and I had the privilege of being co-therapist with him in two groups over the next two years. For me it was the ultimate in accolades. In addition to being valuable for the clients, it was fun and an excellent learning experience, as The Man was particularly gifted in the art of group therapy. This experience gave me the courage for my next undertaking.

Sex and Love Addictions Anonymous had been doing well over the years but had come to a halt by early 1999. I felt I had paid my dues, and it was time to move on. But I had been feeling for a while that there were issues particular to men, which perhaps were of primary concern but which were not being addressed. And so I started Men's Group for the Millennium, a group specifically for men, to deal with issues such as sexual addiction, sexual abuse and the objectification of self and others. Week after week I was humbled as these men took risks and dared to reframe their sexuality into a newer model in which they could be free from addiction. Those that were pornography addicts, threw away their stash, and we supported them through their loss. If, or rather when, a member downloaded more images, we helped him to recreate sobriety in an atmosphere free of judgement. This was not a group to tiptoe around issues. Each member was encouraged to express his feelings frankly and without censure, to get down and dirty, so to speak. In an all-male group where expressing emotion was encouraged, of course there was always the possibility of anger or aggression coming to the fore. But there was only one incident when I felt under threat.

I remember the night it happened. There were five of us in group, including Morose Martin, Captain Recovery, Tony, and our newest member, Ronnie the Newcomer. The group members were talking about their elusive search for love and intimacy, when Ronnie piped up with, 'Well I'm married and I love my wife and I know what intimacy is.' He then expounded on this happy state of affairs for the next five minutes. Incidentally, Ronnie was with us because he had been bust for ongoing pornography addiction.

When he had finished pontificating, I said, 'Ronnie, I feel the need to challenge you. I believe your primary relationship is with your pornography.' I had barely finished when he leaned forward toward me and started to shout at me and wag his finger in my face. I sat there, trembling. He shoved his chair back, screeching it against the floor, and shouted, 'I don't need this shit' and tried to leave the group.

I managed to find my voice and half-whispered, 'Ronnie, I understand that this is difficult for you. But I'm hoping you're going to stay.' This was echoed by all the members, even Morose Martin, who was usually too depressed to find the energy to contribute much. Ronnie found the courage to stay and I was able to share my fear with him and tell him that I thought he might have hit me. It turned out to be a major turning point for him as he owned the fact that he bullied 'real' women, like his wife, and admitted how hard it was for him to hear how scared I had been. I daresay that the incident might have been even more significant for me. Back at the treatment centre, when I had been 'the counsellor you love to hate', I had been quite fearless in my challenging of people and had been unfazed by their anger and rage. This event made me realise that it was more like I'd been completely disconnected from my feelings. Rather than being courageous, I had dissociated in order to deal with my very real fear of anger and fury. Much later I was to learn that this fear stemmed from childhood; my father had been prone to rage attacks (this I learnt from my sister Ca) and I have some distant memories of a man going ballistic. Recovery was full of surprises.

I had the honour of facilitating men's group for the next four years. The men would come and go, but the underlying essence of the group would remain as we tackled difficult issues. Very soon after the start of Men's Group, I took another leap of faith and began what would be a wondrous voyage as a women's group, From Princess to Queen, was born. This group created a protected space for some spectacularly brave women who trekked their way from the wildernesses of their own unexplored femininity through their fears around sexuality, intimacy and commitment. It was not a journey for the faint-hearted. I specifically remember one evening in which we had started to deal with sexuality and as I mentioned 'vagina', these hard-core chicks, who could talk about cunts and pussies and feel nothing, became shy and embarrassed. One of them burst into tears as she admitted her pain in becoming more present in her body. I held the space as they pushed through their self-imposed limitations and together we laughed and cried our way into a new kind of healing.

It was at around this time that my search for meaning drew me to books with titles that in the past I might have been contemptuous of, like *Out of the Darkness into the Light* by Gerald Jampolsky, which offered me an alternative way of viewing the world. I absolutely wept when I read *A Return to Love* by Marianne Williamson. Her words, so simple but profound in their authenticity, evoked a very powerful response and created a total paradigm shift. Although I read widely, I tried not to fall into 'shoo wah' madness land, as I discovered that there were many self-appointed gurus out there in self-help city selling weird and wondrous concepts that purported to take me to nirvana. It was an opportunity to test out my boundaries of discernment and mostly I succeeded, although there are a few books that sit at the back of a cupboard and every now and again I'll unexpectedly catch sight of them and think 'Christ Jo, what were you thinking?'

Neale Donald Walsch's *Conversations with God* series does not fall into this category. When I first came across his books, I was immediately spellbound by the messages contained in them. I had no problem believing that his words were channelled, and they took me to another level of consciousness. As my changes became more internally integrated, I no longer wanted to be the kind of therapist that I had become. I wanted to approach my work more from a space of love. I was no longer happy being the counsellor that 'everyone loves to hate'. So I started to prepare myself for leaving the treatment centre. It was time to move on. Borrowing a line from *A Return to Love* that had always exhilarated me, 'Faith isn't blind, it's visionary', I decided to go into private practice.

# 14

# The full truth

Finding Bella Vita Healing Centre was a synchronistic moment in my recovery. Darren and I had been struggling to find the right space for my private practice – the places we went to see were too cold, too clinical, too far out, too unprofessional, too something, and I was becoming despondent. Then one day I saw an ad in the local press which read 'Rooms available at Healing Centre'. It looked interesting so I showed it to Darren. 'Wow, how bizarre,' was his response. 'I was at a lecture there last night! And I spoke to a woman called Bev, who told me she had rooms to rent. Why don't you call her! I phoned immediately and arranged to see her within an hour.

Bev was beautiful, tall and Mediterranean-looking with long, curly brown hair. She explained that she was building on a new therapy room as we spoke. I paid her a deposit there and then, and the room was mine. I then drove straight back to the treatment centre and resigned.

Compared to where I had come from, Bella Vita was like being on another planet, a quiet planet and one in which my dreams came true. Bella Vita was a Reiki centre with three Reiki practitioners, including Bev, who also ran training groups. Bev was famous for her Reiki and Reiki training, and there were always about two to three courses running at any given time. In addition to the Reiki, individuals and companies hired the premises from Bev for anything from teaching yoga to meditation courses. Four times a year a fair was held, featuring the various residents' services and products, such as aromatherapy massages, metaphysical counselling, new-age books and precious stones. I always found fabulous crystals to add to my growing collection of amethysts and rose quartz.

Another of the centre's residents was Gabriel the angel dog, who belonged to Bev. He used to come in and sit on one of my chairs during my therapy sessions. What a beautiful dog – I still miss him terribly, although I don't tell that to Mignon! I adored him being there, and my clients loved it. He made them feel safe and calm.

My first few months at Bella Vita were blissful and so good for my soul. Soon after arriving I approached Patricia, one of the Reiki therapists, about doing sessions with her, and within no time I was a devotee of this ancient modality. I was so inspired that I also signed up for one of Bev's training groups. What I liked about the course was that it wasn't some weekend workshop wonder, but a serious, in-depth course run over eight weeks. There were courses ranging from Reiki One to Advanced Reiki to Master's in Usui Reiki, as well as separate courses for Karuna and Lightarian Reiki. I liked that the courses required serious commitment and application.

And so work and life continued to be idyllic, until one day it was time for the moment of truth; the session with Patricia which uncovered my sexual abuse. What happened in Patricia's room that afternoon came as a complete shock. I remember lying on the bed afterwards, feeling terribly cold and wondering if I'd ever feel warm again. I couldn't stop crying, not just that afternoon but for weeks thereafter. It was some years before I would learn about the regenerative nature of tears. Back then it felt like the tears would never stop.

As the weeks following the revelation turned into a fortnight and then a month, I walked around in a permanent state of nausea. I carried anti-emetics everywhere and would go to extraordinary lengths to avoid throwing up. Emotionally and physically I was still a wreck. It was as if I was experiencing exactly what I'd dissociated as a young child in the present. And it was excruciating. The whole experience was reminiscent of being back in rehab and going through withdrawal. In a sense, I was detoxing; this time expelling dormant feelings and memories. And as my cells released all their septic contents, I was understandably physically uncomfortable. But I knew that this was an important part of my process. So I soldiered on, consoling myself that this was pain for growth as opposed to pain for pain's sake. Every turning point that I had reached on my recovery journey had been preceded by huge amounts of pain, and clearly this was no exception. And while I didn't believe that that suffering was a prerequisite for transformation, personally it had always proved to be a powerful agent of change.

Yet painful as it all was, I was grateful that I was accessing these memories then, as opposed to during my first years in recovery. The reasons were twofold. Firstly, having been clean for a few years, I was able to see what had happened to me as a piece of the puzzle, whereas in early recovery I suspect that I would have been tempted to define and label the abuse as the puzzle itself and become stuck in an old pattern of martyrdom. Secondly, I am not sure that, before then, my foundation would have been solid and grounded enough to go through this without returning to the use of drugs and/or alcohol. Once again I was struck by the timing of the universe, which reinforced my belief that there are no mistakes, no coincidences and everything is as it should be.

On the subject of pain, one morning, on an impulse, I found myself at a tattoo shop in Sandton having my nose pierced. Oh my

God! Had I been aware of how sore it was going to be, I am unconvinced that I would have suffered through it, even though I had secretly desired a nose ring for the longest time. While I do not wish to become too reductionist as to what it represented, I guess it was in part an act of rebellion, just less harmful than my previous self-mutilation! But it also represented change and new beginnings. There were mixed reactions from my family – mostly shock and horror. But I absolutely loved it. And as soon as was possible, I swapped the standard stud for an exquisite, especially designed jewel – a pearl nestled in a gold casing. I had never been particularly interested in jewellery before but now I thrilled at being adorned and decorated, and especially at a time when everything seemed so heavy in my life. It added a welcome if somewhat frivolous and lighthearted energy.

As a counsellor, I was obliged to be in ongoing supervision, and I was fortunate to have Zen, whom I saw once a week. She was wonderfully containing while I was going through all this. I remember telling her during one of our sessions that I realised I'd always 'known' about the abuse, but my mind has been truly magnificent in its efforts to protect me and keep me safe. She agreed but also pointed out, 'Jo, I must warn you that one normally finds the easier things come up first.' She was right.

Over the weeks following the uncovering of my abuse I continued to have flashbacks, reliving those events or rather experiencing them for the first time since I had completely repressed all memories of what had happened. I saw the room again, that cot, my blanket, a shadowy figure approaching, at first vague, then more specific. I saw increasingly graphic and horrific images; penis in tiny little baby mouth, vagina exposed and sexualised at such an early age, penis and little tongue, penis and fingers entwined around baby girl body. And then one day I saw the most shocking thing of all. The identity of the shadowy figure, my abuser. It was my father.

# 15

## Closure

At first I put off telling anyone. I wasn't ready to speak to either of my brothers about my abuse, and as much as I wanted to tell my big sister, Ca, I hesitated. Would she believe me? It is hard not to feel angry when I think of how I questioned myself. I suppose my doubt was one of the legacies of growing up in a family in which denial was the order of the day.

But the knowledge was too much to bear on my own, and one night, a few weeks after the Reiki session, I phoned Ca.

'Ca, I need to talk to you.'

She got a fright at the tone in my voice. 'Well Sid's at a dinner, why don't you come over?'

I didn't need to be asked twice, and drove over there in record time. As we sat down in the comfort of her sitting-room, I got straight to the point.

'I've been sexually abused. By Mervyn.'

At this stage so many thought were zigzagging through my brain that I had given myself a headache. I scanned her face for any sign of cynicism or judgement and found none. Instead, her words were gentle and full of compassion.

'Gee, Jo! You've had a shit life.'

Hugely relieved, I leaned back in the chair and started to cry again. As the tears streamed down my face, Ca started talking about what she remembered from that time.

'Well, Ma and Mervyn separated and then got back together in the year before you were born, so you must have been the result of that reunion. And then Mervyn left when you were four, so it must have happened within those few years.'

As we spoke, the unreal started to become real, and I was suddenly grateful that I was no longer alone with all this shit in my head. We were discussing possibilities, no, definitely certainties, and I started to feel less victimised. I left to go home feeling a bit more knowledgeable and a lot more contained. It was amazing what support could do; my healing had begun.

After that first conversation, Ca and I spoke often and our relationship shifted as we began to open up to one another and become closer. As the mother of two beautiful young women, Janey and Suzie, Ca had a calming maternal energy. I felt comfortable and safe in her home. Her husband, Sid, whom she met in 1973 through a mutual friend of both our and his parents, was also a great support to me, giving Ca and me space as we talked for hours and hours.

Ca told me what it had been like to be the eldest in the family and explained her relationships with my mother, Mervyn and Johnnie. It was fascinating. It was almost as if we had grown up in different families. Besides being the 'good girl', which meant that she interacted with our parents differently, she could remember all sorts of things which I had forgotten. One day she shared with me one of her memories.

'I was about seven or eight,' she explained, 'and I was doing handstands from the wall straight onto the grass, and I fell and broke my arm. But I was too terrified to go and tell Ma because she was playing bridge, and you never disturbed her while she was playing bridge, ever! I waited for perhaps an hour and a half until they were having tea and then went in. One of the bridge ladies turned to Ma and said, "Oh shame Dee, I never knew that Carolyn had a deformed arm!"' As awful as this was, we laughed hysterically at those demented women.

On a more serious note, Ca told me about Mervyn and Ma's constant fighting. 'They both had vicious tempers,' she said, 'and there were plenty of times when we ran down the road to Granny and Grampa for refuge;' I had been there too, but, of course, I couldn't remember any of this.

One night Ca suggested that maybe I needed to speak to someone who might remember more about our childhood, from a different perspective. My choices were limited in that not many of our family members were still alive – my grandparents and parents had all passed away and my aunt, The Queen, was no longer living in South Africa. Eventually we decided that the best and only place to start would be Port Elizabeth, the windy city of my birth, and the place where the abuse had happened. We would visit our step-grandmother on our father's side, Auntie Bee. Perhaps she would remember something from the past that would help to fill in some of the gaps in my memory. I also hoped that visiting our old family home might trigger some repressed feelings, which I would need to process if I was to achieve some sort of closure. Of course the ultimate act of closure would have been to confront Mervyn, but sadly he had passed away from lung cancer in May 1993, my last year of using.

So a few months later I found myself sitting buckled up on an aeroplane on my way to Port Elizabeth to face my demons, with Ca in the seat next to me. My thoughts were racing and I was feeling scared and vulnerable. I was grateful to be with Ca, whose energy is always very calming. She would be my protector over the next thirty-six hours.

From the time that I was five years old, every July I would fly down to PE, on my own, to visit both sets of grandparents. While there, I would spend large amounts of time with Auntie Beryl, or Bee. Auntie Bee was the second wife of my paternal grandfather, Grampa Harry (or HB, as he was universally known).

Auntie Bee had always been an icon for me. I adored her in childhood. Through my little girl eyes, she was this goddess with the silvery voice, beauty and glamour personified. Her impressive wardrobe was put together by Seymour, who was then a celebrated couturier to the mink and manure set of the day. Her signature perfume was Joy by Patou, the smell of which still today is redolent of luxuriant times gone by. Her face was always painted, if maybe a bit over done, and her eyeshadow was one of a kind that she ordered especially from Europe. It was an emerald green that would have been grotesque on anyone else, but it suited her rather Junoesque looks. She let me go through her wardrobe and we talked endlessly about cosmetics. When I was about nine or ten years old, she bought me my first pair of high heels. They were my prized possession. My mother was not impressed.

Each July I would arrive at the then H F Verwoerd Airport and both sets of grandparents would be waiting to meet me off the plane. It was quite exciting. After all, in those days flying was still quite magical. And certainly to a young girl who lived in a world of illusion and fantasy.

My maternal grandparents were reasonably well off, but Mervyn's father, HB, was seriously wealthy. He and his brother Emmanuel had been the founders of Shatterprufe, which later became Plate Glass. HB drove a sleek, black Lincoln with electric windows, which, for the times, was quite revolutionary. It looked a bit like a hearse. There was only one other car like it, driven by Mr Oddiesbodies – well, that was the name of his business. For years I thought Mr O was the local undertaker, only to discover, to my chagrin, that he owned a huge truck company. I much preferred my original belief.

Up until my mid-twenties, HB continued to support me financially and bailed me out on more than one occasion as I lurched from one financial crisis to the next. Intoxicated by money and the acquisition of material things, I would make indulgent purchases in an effort to make myself feel better and then, when I couldn't pay my rent, in desperation I would call Gramps at the office and abjectly plead my case. He would always say yes, and I would fly down to PE to graciously accept the cash. I was always grateful and contrite, promising him that I wouldn't go on a spending spree ever again. But there was always a next time, and a time after that. And naturally, it would be our little secret. Nobody could know, especially not Auntie Bee.

No one in our family liked Auntie Bee – they saw her as a gold digger. Certainly The Queen, Gramps's daughter and our aunt, detested her. And my own mother, Devora (Dee), was also not her most ardent fan. They definitely resented her spending HB's fortune. I would take part in these alliances later on in my life, but as a child I needed my own ally, and one of these was Auntie Bee. It was she and I against my mother. Auntie Bee always treated me with respect and took me seriously from the start. This meant a great deal to someone whose nickname in the family was 'Moaning Minnie'. The other alliance I had was with my maternal grandmother, Rona. She was affectionate with me and always listened carefully to what I had to say. I think she felt special in that I chose to spend time with her.

Auntie Bee and HB were always going off on world cruises to exotic places. They would return to PE via Johannesburg and spend an evening with us. I would eagerly await their arrival, in anticipation of the gifts they always brought. HB would give us money and Auntie Bee would have bought us something completely useless but decorative and expensive, bearing testimony to the faraway lands they had just visited.

'So did I tell you that Auntie Bee wants to drive us around while we are there?' Ca asked, jolting me out of my reverie. 'Christ, you are joking!' I answered, cringing at the thought. 'She must be eighty-five at least, and how bad must her shaking be by now?' We both started to giggle. Of course, it was no laughing matter, but we cackled hysterically as past images and memories flooded into our minds of Bee and her 'shaking'.

Bee had always had a tremor in her hands. Never mind a tremor, it was more like major quaking. We, that is the family, thought she had Parkinson's disease, but she would no more have acknowledged illness than fly to the moon. So because it was not acknowledged, it simply did not exist. Watching her shake, rattle and roll while she poured a cup of tea and then handed it over was painful to see. That she never spilled a drop said much about her steely resolve to control even that which was beyond her grasp.

Once we'd calmed down, Ca said, 'No, of course not, I've rented a car. We'll collect it at the airport.' Relieved, I asked her about our immediate plans and we discussed our itinerary as the plane came to a somewhat bumpy halt. As we alighted from the aircraft we were nearly knocked over by gale force winds. 'Welcome to the friendly city!' I said to Ca. It was as though the gods of the winds were giving me fair warning that this was going to be a tumultuous journey, emotionally speaking.

En route to the car, we walked through the airport foyer, and suddenly I was struck by a memory. On my previous visits to PE there had always been flower sellers here displaying what seemed like hundreds of bouquets of proteas wrapped in cellophane. I love flowers, and during my life have surrounded myself with as many as possible, always feeling inspired and uplifted by the presence of fresh blooms. But I loathe proteas. So much so that I cannot bear to be anywhere near them, and on the few occasions when they have appeared in arrangements that have been sent to me, I have been compelled to remove them forthwith! I had never really questioned this aversion until that day. Remembering these mummified arrangements, I realised that what they reminded me of was this city, the place where I had been so violated. Without knowing it, I had subconsciously associated these flowers with my abuse.

Shaken by these disturbing memories, I managed to gather myself enough to collect our luggage and we made our way to our hotel, which was right on the beach front and had a casino in its back garden. We decided that we would drive out to our old family home before going to Auntie Bee.

As Ca stopped the car outside the house I battled to keep the tears at bay. It was impossible to shake the sense of dread I felt being there, knowing what had happened in that building. The house seemed smaller than I had envisaged it, yet it was far from benign in what it represented. I tried to reassure myself that everything was okay, that I was safe, but it all seemed terribly overwhelming to the adult child that I was. As a myriad conflicting emotions raced through my mind, I knew better than to try to process any of them. I just allowed them space and tried to have faith in the process that had brought me this far. This is what I had come here for, after all – to experience these feelings. No matter how disturbing or painful, they had to be felt. Slightly calmer, I exhaled and we decided to get out of the car and walk around the house. We approached it with some trepidation, feeling a bit like we were casing the joint. I saw the window of the top floor room. Ca suggested, 'Why don't we knock on the door and ask if we can look around?' This idea sent me into an absolute panic and suddenly it was all too much and I had to get out of there, immediately. In any case, it was almost time for us to meet with Bee.

As we drove away, I was once again filled with gratitude that Ca was with me and that I did not have to deal with all these resurfacing feelings alone. In addition to her calming presence, my ability to dissociate created distance from all the obscenities that took place at number three Malta Road Glendinningvale, and so by the time we arrived at Bee's apartment I was suitably composed.

Phyllis let us in and waved us through to the lounge. Phyllis had been with Auntie Bee for decades, going back to HB's days, and she and Bee had a love/hate relationship. Bee was waiting to greet us and I was shocked at how she looked. As always, she was dressed to the nines, immaculately coiffed, if a little mauve, and, unbelievably, still wearing stiletto heels at the grand age of eighty-five. But, where once statuesque, she had diminished decidedly; she had in a sense become a caricature of herself. Later on, we remarked rather unkindly that she looked like Minnie Mouse on heels!

Bee knew who Ca was immediately, but didn't recognise me and had to be reminded who I was. After speaking for a while, we realised that Auntie Bee had become a bit gaga. Suddenly I felt sad, whether for her or for me, I'm unsure. Saddened by the vagaries of life that ended up with Beryl, at eighty-five, completely alone, bouncing around in this big but charmless apartment. It struck me that Bee had gone batty in order to survive. Maybe it was a way for her to escape the constrictions of her life. Perhaps everything had become too much and so, to avoid her painful reality, she had stoically fallen into semi-senility. I badly wanted to interrogate her on family secrets, to ask her questions about Mervyn and The Queen and even Sophie, in the vain hope that her answers would help to make sense of the senseless. But sadly, I realised, reluctantly, that it was never going to happen. Whatever she knew, she would continue her seeming vow of silence and, sphinx-like, carry riddles and mysteries to her grave.

We had planned to go out for lunch, and once again, Bee offered to drive us. Keeping straight faces, we declined graciously and took her to an Italian restaurant close to our hotel. Luncheon was fairly tense as Bee still shook hectically, at times looking like she was going through a full-blown case of the DTs. Naturally, we pretended not to notice. Also, as she became less and less lucid, conversation turned into an art form. Ca managed to decipher her confused speech admirably, though, enough to keep up a conversation with her.

'So Auntie Bee, I think you saw Sid recently?' And Auntie Bee responded, 'I don't know Sid but I think I know your husband, he was always very kind to me.'

I could not keep track, however, and was feeling increasingly down. It was distressing to see my iconic figure like this, and I was bitterly disappointed by the fact that I was not going to find out anything from her and might never know any more than I did right now. Wishing I still smoked, I moodily picked at a piece of cake. Then, out of a desperate need to connect with this woman, I shared with her how she had played such a vital role in my childhood. My words seemed to get through, and in her still silvery voice, she tinkled, 'Thank you, Jody darling.' Turning to Ca she said, 'You know, Ca darling, I could never understand why Jo would want to spend so much time with me. I always felt so honoured.' Our souls touched for the briefest of moments and for the first time on that trip I felt less hopeless.

After a few hours, it was time to take Bee back. We drove her home and I found myself making all sorts of promises about future contact, which I knew I would never keep. Speeding away both from Bee's life and all the feelings that had been aroused that day, I said to Ca, 'I'm finished!' She was feeling the same way, but we nevertheless decided to do a little more investigation into the old neighbourhood. En route, we discussed our session with Beryl and I brought up her step-daughter, and our aunt, The Queen. Bee had mentioned how lovely it was that 'The Queen and I speak often and are very close'. I'd been surprised at this as they had been sworn enemies for all of their lives. Of course, not to each other's faces, and never in public, where everything was about appearances and image and behaving comme il faut. That's how we operated in my family. No wonder most of us were a bit unbalanced!

As we drove, I saw the place where our corner café used to be, and, with great excitement, I screeched at Ca to stop the car. We stayed there a while, the car idling, while I recalled the shop I used to go to so often, the sweets I would buy; Wilson's buttermilk, liquorice toffee and those tangy pink sweets – I forget their name. After summoning up these candy visions of delight from yesteryear, and feeling more energised, we cruised along to Granny Rona's old house. Here the thoughts and feelings of the past were bittersweet. I had loved Granny Rona and, certainly, she had championed my cause over the years, but I realised that I had never really known her. I knew certain facts about her, but it was not the same as knowing her on a personal level. I knew my grandfather Grisha even less; he was around, but at a distance. What I did know was that he'd had a fierce temper. As the story goes, my mother used to have beautiful, long hair down past her waist, and when she was sixteen, she went and had it chopped off. Grisha was so consumed with rage that he thrashed the living daylights out of her. This story always left me feeling disquieted. Maybe it explained some of my mother's issues around men and the inability of her antennae to pick up on abuse in her marriage.

Mission accomplished for the day, and feeling somewhat wasted, we hastened back to the hotel, intent on chilling and unwinding for a while. An hour or so later, feeling slightly more invigorated due more to the restorative powers of a luxurious, hot bath than any lifting of my spirits, I joined Ca in the hotel lounge, and we toasted our survival with orange juice while deciding on our next movements. I was still feeling vulnerable and I craved childhood food. 'Pizza,' I pleaded, hoping that Ca was not in the mood for anything more epicurean this evening. Happily we agreed on pizza and because the casino, being a second away, was beckoning, we resolved to go and have a look-see after our meal.

After my childish appetite had been sated, it was time for more grown-up pleasures. We found our way into the gambling floor and everything changed instantly. It was a bit like stepping into a crack den. A very glitzy and showy crack den, maybe, but nonetheless it had 'using' energy. Normally I would have been repelled. But tonight was different; tonight I was going to indulge and be a bit careless with my recovery! I was feeling fearless.

Ca gave me a few hundred rand and armed with my cash I started staking out the slot machines to see which one was going to be lady luck that night. I watched at first and, like most voyeurs, I was guarded in my infatuation. After a while, it was time to become more adventurous, so I began to play the field, flirting here and there. But as my money was gobbled up voraciously, I decided it was time to get mean. And then I spied a machine that had 'dark and dangerous' written all over it. Seduced from afar, I went over, eased my way into an uncomfortable chair and began my own Mata Hari number. The next thing, lights flashed, bells rang and I'd won. My heart leaped with excitement. I wanted more and more. For the next few hours there was only the machine and I. Nothing and nobody existed outside of us. All the pain and hurt that I'd been feeling disappeared and I was in another world. I won some, I lost some … I didn't care. As long as this glorious nothingness could continue, life was sweet. And I was sure of this; if someone tried to come between my machine and me, I would have killed that person! That's how powerful I felt. Ultimately I gave my last twenty rand to the object of my obsession, which devoured it within seconds and that was that.

The addict in me screamed, 'Come on, you can't stop now, you're on a roll!' and all sorts of other lies, but it was over. I was done. Only then, as I came back to my senses, did I stop to look at what was going on around me. The casino was crowded with what seemed like very ordinary people, all determined to win big, and in some cases probably willing to go to any lengths to follow the trail of fool's gold. Although the powers that be had done their best to create an ambience of glitter and festivity, it seemed forced, and there was more than a hint of desperation in the air.

I realised that, left to my own devices, I could easily have become a gambling addict. As I felt and saw some of the misery that was palpable in these halls, I was tremendously thankful for being clean and sober. My gratitude made me feel better, and I went to find Ca, who had come away with some winnings. And so, content with the night's entertainment, we returned to our much-awaited beds and passed out.

I woke up the next morning and, unsurprisingly after the previous night's carry on, felt like I'd been using. My body was stiff and my head sore, groggy and resistant to the thought of another day in paradise. My Narcotics Anonymous Nazi voice told me, 'Last night was a relapse and if you are not careful you'll use again and die!' 'Yeah, yeah, yeah,' I muttered wearily to myself. 'Not now, please! Can we deal with this later?' Pushing aside the eternal monkey on my back that is addiction, I got up and groomed myself for the day.

Watching the sea from our hotel window, pictures flashed unbidden of December holidays as a child. I remembered how our family would drive down each year to PE and spend every day, weather permitting, at the beach. I used to love swimming in the sea. I would stay in the water for as long as I could, my body becoming all shrivelled up. It was magnificent.

Of course, other memories intruded which were less pleasant. An older me, hugely self-conscious of my heavy body in a bathing suit, wanting to go and swim but being too insecure to walk from where I sat to the water in case people mocked me. Sometimes I wouldn't even take my shirt off – I would lie down and swelter and suffer until it was time to go home. As these snapshot frames ran through my head, Ca suggested we go for a walk along the waterfront. We set off and, once again, the windy city was living up to its well-earned title. Howling winds were blowing down, making it difficult to remain standing. Determined to go for our stroll along the promenade, we crossed the road and strode forth. We were no match for the elements, however, and after a short time I was forced to recognise my own limitations – something that I've struggled with repeatedly in recovery – and we turned around and almost leopard crawled back to our temporary haven.

Safely under shelter, and discussing our agenda for the day, which included a trip to the Jewish cemetery to visit my grandparents' graves, I suddenly decided that I could not bear another minute in this town. Our flight was booked for late afternoon but that seemed like centuries away. Ca was of similar mind, being keen to get back to her family, and immediately called the airline to change the reservations. Thankfully, we were given two seats on the next flight, which left in two hours. Relieved by this news, I felt my spirits lift and I trusted that I had experienced what I needed to in terms of my process. Anything more at this point, I thought, would be a journey of self-hatred rather than self-loving.

We got our stuff together in record time and were on our way to the airport within fifteen minutes. By then, it was raining too, so it was with absolutely no regrets that I bade farewell to the oppressive, gloomy Port Elizabeth. The skies were heavily overshadowed, concealing mysteries that might forever remain hidden. But I knew that more would be revealed in time to come. What I would gratefully access much later on was how restorative this trip actually was, and if the wind was the healing power of the spirit then the gods had definitely been smiling down benevolently all the while.

# 16

## Meltdown I

The next few years were spent in love and light as I grew my practice and my counselling room became a sanctuary where my clients felt safe and contained. Bev was one of the most powerful women that I have ever met, and her energy infused the centre with an air of integrity. I continued to do more advanced courses in Reiki, and Darren started to work there too. He set up his own practice at the centre, offering energy healing, which was supportive to talk therapy.

Darren had come a long way to get to this point. Towards the end of high school he didn't really know what he wanted to do with his life. I think his father suggested hotel school but he wasn't keen. And he wasn't interested in going to university even though he obtained a university pass. Darren started selling clothes at taxi ranks while in the meantime he began smoking copious amounts of weed, which I knew nothing about. Of course, the irony does not escape me that here I was, the great addiction counsellor, and Darren was smoking weed right under my nose! After a year of this, his life started falling apart, and he ran away to Israel. That didn't last too long and he came back and started working in a graphic design shop, which he really enjoyed, and decided that he wanted to study graphic design. But he was still smoking and still not dealing with his issues. At the age of twenty he thought there must be something more, and tried to kill himself on an overdose of Valoid (an anti-nausea tablet – a toxic dose is three and he had taken a whole box). The night he took them he went missing. I was beside myself. We, that is, my family, his friends and I, could not find him. I honestly thought he was dead and I was literally keening, I was so distressed. Eventually my sister found him at the very end of the complex's gardens (it was very dark down there) and he was frothing at the mouth. Fortunately we got him to the hospital and they looked after him there. He had mirrored my own actions, and as had happened to me eventually, his suicide attempt turned out to be his personal transformation. He started seeing an amazing metaphysical counsellor and began reading metaphysical books from a shamanic perspective, and on his travels in America and Australia he first heard about Reiki. He did a Reiki course in Australia and on returning to Johannesburg, enrolled in one of Bev's courses.

So the two of us were working side by side, and life was sweet. I was still having flashbacks to my abuse every now and again, but I was feeling more accepting about where I was at. I remember reading a book around that time called *Memory and Abuse* and coming across this sentence, 'She avoided food that reminded her of oral sex, including white sauces and mayonnaise.' As I saw these words, I leapt off the chair, ran out of the room and vomited – although nothing but bile came up. As I've mentioned before, to vomit is the end of the world for me. I knew instantly what had been a mystery for years; the reason why I had never been able to eat anything white from the time I was little. I had already seen images of my childhood oral sexual abuse but had never linked this with my aversion to throwing up. Despite the feelings of disgust this discovery aroused in me, I was pleased in that it added more meaning to who I had become. It was another reclaimed memory.

Everything was about to change, though, as in July 2004 I began to descend into a darkness like nothing I had experienced before. It was a kind of depression, or more of a morbid melancholia, yet at the same time I could have moments of ebullience. I felt strange sensations in my body and prickly touches from unknown assailants; in short, I felt like I was going insane. Looking back, it is clear that I was in the grip of what is known as a bipolar mixed episode with psychotic features, but my denial around the extent of my illness was so entrenched that I didn't even know such a thing existed.

I had been diagnosed with bipolar type II, which is a gentler, watered down version of bipolar I. Despite this diagnosis, I had never taken the illness seriously, and in my mind had been mostly stable for years. Little ups, little downs – some irritability, but all quite 'normal' and manageable. Or so I'd thought. I'm not so sure anymore, and Darren tells me that over the years my 'moods were frightening'. I guess having been through so much with my various addictions, I did not want to face up to the fact that there was more to deal with, and was therefore unwilling to admit to myself the severity of my disorder. Another reason I was unable to acknowledge the full implications of my illness had to do with the stigma attached to mental disease. For me it was always easier to say that I was an addict than to admit to having bipolar mood disorder. I felt that addiction was more mainstream and 'accepted' by society than mental illness, and that there was still much work to be done in terms of creating awareness and opening up dialogue around psychiatric illnesses like bipolar.

With this agenda in mind, earlier that year I had started a twelve-step recovery support group called Double Trouble. Similar to Alcoholics Anonymous and Narcotics Anonymous, this meeting had been running in the USA for years and was a space for people who had a chemical dependency or process addiction as well as a psychiatric illness. A great many addicts and alcoholics have a dual diagnosis, meaning that they, like me, have an addiction as well as some psychiatric 'other'. Double Trouble provided a space where people could come and talk about all this 'other', discuss the effects of their meds and their impact on recovery, and learn more about the illness through other persons.

Initially, it was quite difficult as a counsellor to divulge my bipolar status to the group members at Double Trouble. My fear, reinforced by the negative voices in my head, was, 'Would clients still trust me as their therapist?' In reality, they were appreciative of my disclosure. It allowed them to feel safe enough to share their own stuff. But as I sat and listened to people talking about their experiences, I would often focus on the differences between us and feel quite pleased with myself and complacent to boot. They would trade gruesome stories about their mania on the one hand while on the other they would become sentimental recalling how much they loved and missed the high of the manic phases. I actually believed, listening to them, that I hadn't ever been truly manic. What planet was I living on!? Clearly my defence mechanisms, which had protected me superbly as a little girl, were still in force. But what had been valuable in childhood had become life threatening, as this ability to deny what was happening meant that my illness was able to continue unfettered, bringing destruction to my life and those around me.

Whatever I was going through that July certainly seemed more intense than the sort of existential crisis I had experienced before. All of my normal remedies crumbled in the face of this new nightmare. In my desperation, and despite Darren trying to be a voice of reason, I sought help from the most bizarre quarters; at one stage I had Wendy the Witch complete with broomstick arriving at my townhouse to cleanse it of all psychic enemies. (As serious as my condition was, Darren and I spent many a moment hysterical in laughter as we recalled the broomstick biddy.) She informed me what steps I would need to take for my further safety. Naturally, all of this came with a hefty price tag, and despite Darren's gentle warnings I was lost in my psychosis as I dutifully bought lavender oil to put on my pillows and tea-tree oil to smear onto the plug sockets to protect me from 'the gathering evil'! It was at this point that, even in my sick state, something clicked, and I managed to dispense of her services, albeit as I was gibbering meaningless mantras to ward off the harmful spirits. But this was not to be the end. My condition, no doubt exacerbated by all the crackpot energies I was exposing myself to, worsened, and I subsequently became convinced that I was possessed. I called in another healer that Darren and I had worked with before and had him perform some kind of energetic exorcism. Obviously it made no difference to my tortured state of mind or the constant tingling sensations that I was experiencing.

Although I had thought about suicide often, it had ceased to be an option because of a new insight I had gained. On the day that I had decided to call the psychiatrist whom I had been working with for a few years to hospitalise me and put me on a drip, I went to see someone who came highly recommended. He explained to me that I was living out a past life in the present, and encouraged me to write letters to my former incarnation in an effort to deal with some of this 'past life' stuff. So with my newfound belief in reincarnation, the idea of killing myself and then having to come back and deal with all this shit again no longer appealed!

I can recall nights lying on a blanket out in the moonlight with Darren giving me Reiki; those were the few tolerable moments I had in the overall agony. It was more than a dark night of the soul, but like everything else in my recovery, it ultimately strengthened me. What I have only really recognised now is that Darren did more than support me through this time; he nursed me through an illness. I'm not sure that this was something a child (albeit a young man of twenty-five) should have to do for a parent, but I honestly feel that I would not have survived those months had it not been for his strength. Thinking of this now, I'm tearful, but these are tears of gratitude at the magnitude of his power and my love for who he is.

I gradually came out of my black jungle warzone, and although

I still left my bedside light on at night for some time after that, I started to feel happy again, little by little. This was fortunate, as by then the healing centre had been sold. Bev had been made an offer she couldn't refuse and was moving to Nelspruit, and Darren and I had moved to an outpatient addiction treatment facility where I was renting rooms. I had my own practice and I also agreed to co-facilitate a group for the owners of the outpatient facility once a week. In the near future I would see clients who had been damaged by all means of crazy new-age offerings, and my own experience gave me the insight into what happens when all reason flies out the window.

A few months later, in stark contrast to some of the 'out there' therapies I had brought into my reality, I experienced an extremely grounded and much-needed ceremony in the form of a sweat lodge. A sweat lodge is a ceremonial sauna in which stones are heated and then placed in a central pit inside the lodge, which resembles an igloo. Inside the lodge, participants make prayers and offerings to the spirit world. I didn't know quite what to expect the first time, but as I sat, preparing my prayer ties, I found myself reconnecting to the power of prayer and started to feel better immediately. Prayer ties were cloths of different colours cut into squares, filled with tobacco and tied to a piece of string. These were left in the sweat lodge as offerings of gratitude. Before entering the lodge I had to remove all jewellery, including my nose piercing, which I was rather reluctant to take out. After the sweat, much as I tried, I couldn't get it back in again, and although initially I was really upset, I came to realise that the piercing had symbolised my abuse and I no longer needed it. It was a bittersweet loss, as I had become attached to my adornment, but in the weeks ahead I would feel lighter without it. Amusingly, within the next week I was flying to Sydney to visit my brother Phil, his wife Jen and their two kids, Jacob and Ruby. The children, having heard about their aunt's infamous piercing, had been waiting with bated breath to see my nose ring. But at the very last minute, it was not to be! We still had the most stunning visit and it was fabulous to see all of them.

How appropriate that part of the process was making way for a new life force to enter. You literally sweated out all your old stuff and left it behind in the lodge, allowing new clean energy to enter – it was a spiritually renewing, transformative shift in consciousness and definitely the most cleansing experience I have ever gone through.

I gradually settled into the new centre but it always felt temporary, as though I was waiting for something else. The premises were spectacularly beautiful, but once again I was renting rooms, on the outside looking in, and I yearned for more. Before I had started at the new centre it had all sounded so idyllic, but in reality I was again reliving the story of my family, complete with alliances and cabals. Although I was helping with their groups once a week, I never felt accepted by the staff at the facility. Part of the problem was that I had been working on my own for three years and had become quite set in my ways. Tuning into other peoples' rhythms and frequencies proved to be quite a challenge. I hadn't realised how difficult I could be, and my need to be 'the best' created tensions and edginess. This was especially evident in the outpatient group which I co-facilitated once a week. The other counsellors, who were permanent members of staff, felt sidelined by me, and confronted me on this, but I paid lip service to their feedback and carried on doing things my way.

We had peer supervision every week, during which we would discuss certain client cases. One day one of the owners offered some negative feedback to all the counsellors, and I took it personally and felt stung, especially because he wasn't even a therapist. I answered, 'I'm not even going to dignify that with a response' in my iciest and haughtiest manner. My ego definitely got in the way, which left me feeling empty and lost. My reactions became childish, and ultimately I withdrew, and stopped doing group for them. Shutting down was so easy for me. I became unfailingly polite and a bit nasty, which of course benefited nobody, least of all me. I was surprised at the ease with which I could turn my back on people, places and things, and feel nothing, but then again I came from a family with a history of emotional cut-offs (for example two sisters in Granny Rona's family did not speak to one another for fifteen years).

As I lugged this heaviness to my supervision session with Zen, my thoughts were, 'Does the work on self ever end?' I knew it was a silly question but I was feeling resistant, which manifested when Zen urged me to go and make amends for some or other of my ungracious behaviours. I did so reluctantly, but my apologies lacked substance because whatever had transpired was never about that person to begin with; it was who he or she represented for me that had triggered my behaviour.

After I had been at the outpatient centre for close to a year, I somewhat impulsively agreed to take part in a television network's series on sex and health. As part of the series, they were doing a segment on sex addiction, and I agreed to tell my personal story as well as talk about my experiences as a practitioner in the field.

Ever since I have been in recovery, I have tried to present sex addiction as a serious illness, but have mostly been a lone pioneering voice in the midst of a society that seems to completely support and enable the addiction. I remember when in 1997 on *Carte Blanche* they aired an American piece on sex addiction and afterwards, Derek Watts turned to Ruda Landman with a look of pure amazement and said, 'Only in America!' By then, my twelve-step group, Sex and Love Addiction Anonymous, had already been in existence in Joburg for three years, and I couldn't wait until the next morning to contact them and inform them of our existence. This led to me as well as a few other members being interviewed by Ruda, and the resulting programme was probably the most thoughtful I have seen. I didn't disclose everything, for instance I didn't talk about the prostitution, but it was enough to create some awareness and offer some solidarity for the thousands of addicts out there who feel so alone, isolated and ashamed.

Perhaps I hoped this programme would have a similar effect to the previous show, and certainly the journalist from the network assured me that my material would be respected and presented in a mature and gracious manner. Thankfully I reserved the right to see the programme before it went out, because I was horrified to see the envisioned final product. It was patronising to say the very least. The balance of the show was all wrong. The subject matter was sensationalised in that the participants chosen were the more extreme cases, people who were seriously dysfunctional, and were not representative of the average person with sexual issues. It effectively marginalised the disease, making its sufferers look really off the wall. In addition, the chosen participants' inability to speak for themselves in a more empowered way allowed the onsite therapist more freedom to discuss and pass judgement on their cases with the host of the show. What was more disturbing was that the programme was targeting an audience who, in my opinion, saw sex addiction as relatively harmless, with an attitude of, 'Well, if you have to have an addiction, then that's the one to have!' The original segment consisted of me giving my story against a background of their onsite therapist interpreting what I was saying to the host of the show, in a patronising way. After I had seen this first copy, I had threatened to pull out completely. After much toing and froing, a fairly tentative compromise was reached and the therapist and the host were banned from commenting on what I had shared. My segment was followed by a woman who had become caught up in a bizarre SMS addiction, and it would have been quite valuable except that it showed her now completely dependent on her shrink who, besides medicating her, seemed to understand little about her addiction and treated her like a naughty child (she was in her thirties), thus leaving her further disempowered. The last piece was a real beauty; it showed a man in the process of being anally fisted by a hooded individual, which might have been glorious for all the voyeurs out there but personally, I thought it was unnecessary and only compounded the show's effect of marginalising sex addiction. Especially since the man in question was unrepentantly addicted to the activity and completely disinterested in stopping, despite major physical consequences. The other outcome of the show was that it allowed many sex addicts who are not as extreme to think, 'You see, I'm not like these freaks, I don't have a problem …' and to slide further down the slippery slopes of denial.

That period of my life wasn't all doom and gloom, however. Even though I had withdrawn from the centre, or perhaps because of this, my own practice was thriving, I was impassioned by my work, and loved that I was doing my own special interest groups, Men's Group for the Millennium and From Princess to Queen. Also, Darren and I had started to talk about opening our own centre. I was turning fifty and it seemed a kind of now-or-never landmark. I had had a dream for some time; I wanted to provide secondary treatment. Secondary treatment facilities are where addicted clients can go after they finish primary treatment for their disease. Primary treatment is usually not longer than three months, and often clients are not ready to face the real world and require more treatment after this. We casually started looking at premises and then all of a sudden we were serious and within months we found the perfect place for in-patient care. Great therapeutic staff came next and then a spending spree of note as we kitted out the house to get it ready for our opening date.

On 1 March 2006 One Life Addiction Treatment Centre opened its doors. We started with one client and after a few weeks we had three. This quiet period was an opportunity to experiment with the programme and tweak it here and there. And then there were more and suddenly we were operational. My energy certainly played an essential role in that it was very strong and containing, but it was Darren's energy that held the centre. I realise that as his mother I am naturally biased, but Darren has a way with people that is beyond anything I have ever come across in my years in the field. He has a patience and tolerance that to my mind is tinged with an angelic brush. At our centre, not only could he make anybody feel comfortable, be it a client or a family member but, very importantly, he could de-escalate levels of anger and violence.

Rightly or wrongly, we challenged standard treatment norms and walked on the wild side of the moon. For instance, in most if not all treatment centres, if you used drugs or drank, you were asked to leave the centre. We took a different view; we tried to keep clients in treatment as much as possible without endangering any of the other clients.

I honestly feel that even though we were open for such a short time, the clients who came through our place were privileged to be part of a uniquely special space, if they were open to it. And many were, who are now shining in their own lives in the real world. And maybe that's enough to know for now. But it was simply a matter of time before I became caught up once again in the dance with Ladymania.

# 17

# Meltdown II

'Ma, is everything okay?' asked Darren. 'Trust me, Da,' I said confidently. 'Everything's fine, I know what I'm doing. It's all good.' It was October 2007 and I was nearing the peak of a manic depressive crisis or, if we want to get clinical, a bipolar manic episode with psychotic features. And I was telling Darren to trust me!

I'm reminded of the fable of the scorpion and the frog in which the scorpion asks the frog to give him a ride on his back across the river. The frog, a bit concerned for his safety, asks the scorpion, 'How do I know that I can trust you not to kill me?' The scorpion replies that it would not be in his interest to kill the frog, because he cannot swim. They negotiate a deal and off they go. Soon enough, the frog feels the sting of the scorpion. He asks him, 'Why?' And the scorpion responds, 'Self-destruction – it's my nature.'

So I was inviting my son to trust a scorpion. In my defence, not that I feel that I deserve one, I did not know that I was in full-blown mania and also, one of the side effects of this disease is impaired insight and judgement – to put it politely. What actually happens is that all self-knowledge, any insight at all, disappears the moment Ladymania comes calling. There is even a clinical name for it; anosognosia – an inability to recognise, acknowledge or act upon a set of symptoms such as those of mania.

One Life had been open a year and a half, and despite the rewards it had been incredibly tough. We had a relatively small facility – we could take in a maximum of thirteen clients at a time. This was great because it allowed us to work with the clients in a hands-on way. Our programme was full and involved lectures, group therapy, art therapy, life skills and yoga, to mention a few of the activities that took place on a daily or weekly basis. For the first six months, therapeutically and administratively, Darren and I managed on our own. Darren gave Reiki sessions to individual clients and meditation teachings to the groups. He understood group process intuitively and was really good at maintaining appropriate boundaries.

Our consulting staff included Dana, our esteemed art psychotherapist, and Karma, our yoga instructor, who also happened to be a social worker and so was quite capable of containing the group. (We had had two teachers before who had been completely trampled over by the clients.) Then there was Dalene, our supervisor, the wise one who kept all of us sane. As young as she was (in her early thirties) she brought wisdom and a lightness of being that invariably shifted the energy of the house into a happier space. Later, as our client base grew, we employed another social worker, Karen, who was a great asset to our team and very loyal to me, and Justine, a young and enthusiastic trainee counsellor.

I was passionate about my profession and felt blessed to work in this field. However, I was putting in longer and longer hours and some of the most basic principles that I learnt in my early years in recovery, had fallen away. I wasn't looking after myself properly. In the twelve-step fellowships we talk about H.A.L.T., which stands for Hungry, Angry, Lonely and Tired. If an addict is feeling any one of these, this indicates that she or he is in a bad place. I was probably feeling all four of these emotions without being aware of it. So it's no surprise that Ladymania came calling with her dance card. At that point, my little red dancing shoes were in my cupboard where they had been for years, but I started to notice them again, taking in their gorgeous shiny heels and diamante buckles and thinking to myself wistfully that it had been a long time ... Did I even remember the steps?

Of course I did. It began with a frisson in the pit of my stomach and then, almost simultaneously, my energy levels started to rise. It was quite subtle in the beginning, but before long I was dancing and twirling around like a whirling dervish, faster and higher until I was dizzy, on and on in my little red shoes. I couldn't stop.

I have always adored the 'Red Shoes' fairytale by Hans Christian Andersen. There was this girl who got adopted by a rich old lady. One day they went on an outing to buy a pair of shoes for the girl, and in one of the shops she spotted these shiny bright red numbers. The girl, who had become quite vain, managed to sneak them past the old lady, who was rather blind. When she wore them to church that Sunday, the congregation were scandalised by their garishness and she was warned never to wear them again. So she put them away in the cupboard, but could not resist taking them out and trying them on from time to time. Then one day, when she put on the forbidden shoes, they took on a life of their own. A curse had been placed on her as a punishment for her vanity, and she could not stop dancing. She tried in vain to take the shoes off but they would not budge. On and on the girl was forced to dance until eventually, in desperation, she had to ask the local executioner to cut off her feet. She ended up a cripple, forever in servitude to the villagers.

For me, the tale is about obsession and losing one's way, two things with which I strongly identify. The old lady I see as my instinctual nature, which was clearly so damaged that I was unable to see how dangerous the shoes were. I didn't recognise the signs – another example of my denial.

I would find, in the middle of facilitating group therapy or delivering a lecture, that I suddenly felt different. When I looked down, sure enough, those little red shoes were on and my feet were twitching and tapping to their own rhythm. I felt quite powerful – very different from feeling empowered. Feeling powerful meant feeling godlike, grandiose. All humility fell away and I was on a mission, zealous in my intent. But then, half an hour or an hour later, I'd be 'me' again. 'Me' was feeling quite emotional (sad and a little euphoric simultaneously), and so I did what any self-respecting bipolar would do. I immediately blamed my medication for not working and sought help in this regard.

Within weeks I was on so many psycho-pharmaceuticals that I'm convinced that I was developing what we called, way back when, 'the thorazine look and shuffle'. You know, when patients are on so much or such high levels of anti-psychotic meds that their faces lose any form of mobility and seem to get frozen in one expression. And their walking becomes this odd motionless yet quite rigid shuffle.

Living up to my earlier potential around psychiatrists, I guess my own unwellness attracted similar energies amongst the professionals I consulted, and by September I had been prescribed, amongst other things, six different anti-depressants. Well, if Ladymania and I were not yet doing the tango on rooftops, it was certainly going to be anytime soon! Put any person who has manic-depressive illness on six anti-depressants and the result is not going to be pretty. Pretty spectacular maybe, but not pretty.

Given what I now know about bipolar, it seems quite bizarre that I was never prescribed a mood stabiliser. I had always been put onto anti-depressants in addition to loads of benzos, but never anything for my high voltage moods. Obviously it didn't help that I drank and used other drugs, but sometimes I wonder if some of that was an unconscious, despairing attempt on my part to regulate my moods.

By early September of 2007 I needed almost no sleep in order to function. I stayed up later and later and decided that I needed to create more lectures, assignments and other material for our in-patients. The truth is that I had enough material to not repeat any teachings for at least a year, but I was on a roll. I wrote feverishly, at every opportunity I got, whether it was 12.30 at night or 5.30 in the morning. I walked around with my exam pad just in case I thought of something. Everything became urgent and had to be completed now. In admiration, one of our social workers said, 'Wow, Jo, I really don't know where you get your energy from!' I loved hearing this. It fed my obsession.

By now the little red shoes were on most of the time. From having been comfortably celibate for ten years, I became all too aware of my sexual energy. Dissatisfied with the way I looked and felt, I started to spend huge amounts of money on clothing for the new me. I put this down to the fact that I was soon turning fifty-two. My appetite for food dissipated and between that and my ascending energy levels, the weight fell off me and I begin to resemble a concentration camp survivor. Of course, at this stage, blinkers firmly in place, I thought I looked stunning and that I was absolutely fine; it was everybody else who had a problem.

And then the event that changed everything. In October I got involved with a client, who after undergoing treatment at our facility had joined our staff. Although I knew I was breaking an ethical code of conduct, my judgement at the time was so impaired that I could not see any problem in what I was doing. Not surprisingly, the affair had disastrous consequences, for my reputation, my relations with staff, and most off all for the client.

Clients' rights to confidentiality and privacy do not allow me to be too specific about what happened, but the crux of the scandal was that the client ended up nearly dying of an accidental overdose from drugs obtained on our premises. The affair became public knowledge, and subtly or outright, I was blamed for what happened – by everyone.

And so, the icon of recovery that I had been for nearly fourteen years had fallen from grace had managed to trash her hitherto impeccable name within months. Even my relationship with Darren became increasingly strained. Because at that stage no one knew that I was having a bipolar meltdown, it was hard for anyone, including Darren, to empathise with me. He thought I was just being bloody-minded. He tried so hard to talk to me, but I just couldn't and wouldn't hear him. It must have been hell for him. I had alienated everyone else and nearly alienated him too.

November was the beginning of the end. Slowly, I started to comprehend that what I had been going through, and was probably still going through, was a bipolar episode. I realised then that this illness was something I needed to start taking very seriously. It was a Sunday and I was driving back from the centre. In desperation, I called Dr P, an excellent psychiatrist and an expert on addiction. We hadn't always agreed over the years but suddenly, he was the only person I felt I could trust. As I listened to the phone ring on the other end, I prayed that he'd answer.

'Hello.' I heard his familiar voice.

'Hi Charles, it's Joanne Brodie here. I'm so sorry to call you on a Sunday.'

And my voice ran on, filling him in as to what had gone down over the last few weeks. I slowed down for a minute and gave him a chance to get a word or two in. And, to my amazement, I heard something that I would never have expected or predicted. I heard compassion and kindness in his voice. It disarmed me completely. Tears welled up and I wanted to fall apart at this man's tenderness. But this was not the time. I made a valiant effort to keep myself together while Dr P explained that he could not see me professionally because we were colleagues and it would be a crossing of boundaries, but he would refer me to a first-rate person immediately. As I pushed the little red button on my cell to end the call, I breathed out deeply and felt a small sense of relief.

# 18

## Aftermath

I had taken the greatest fall of my recovery and maybe my life. I felt a bit like Humpty Dumpty, unsure if anyone would be able to put me together again. The last few weeks at One Life were hideous. I had lost control of the group and seemed to lurch from one crisis to the next as the clients ran riot. I tried my best to work but it was exceptionally difficult under the circumstances. Some staff members supported me but others felt they couldn't, which I understood (though maybe not immediately!). As sick as I was, I knew somewhere in the recesses of my mind that we wouldn't be able to keep our doors open, but I was not quite ready to acknowledge this.

I might have stopped dancing on ceilings but I was far from out of the woods. My moods were choppy and I alternated between trying to be more okay than I really was and lashing out at everyone around me. I would frequently dissolve in tears and be unable to stop crying. Nobody could stand to be around me for long, to the point that the staff asked me to stay at home, which I tried, but I just couldn't bear to be at home with myself, so before long I convinced Darren to let me come back. He and I still were still barely on speaking terms, for which I now take full responsibility, but then I was furious with him and couldn't understand why he was being so unreasonable.

Eventually my brother-in-law Sid mediated and helped me to see that it was best to close the centre, both financially and for my emotional wellbeing. And so we shut our doors on 30 November 2007. Though I was in shock over the closure, there was another part of me that was hugely relieved that the drama was over. I felt like I'd been holding my breath for an age and could finally exhale.

A few days later, I made my way to my new shrink, Dr Wellness. I immediately felt safe with this man who was so, and I really hate this word, 'normal'. He calmly and quietly went about the business of mending me and 'rationalising' my meds, which is polite speak for 'he threw most of the offending crap out the bloody window'. For the first time in my life, I was properly diagnosed and treated, and over the next few weeks I started to feel a little better, enough to get through the next few months, which involved moving homes and starting a whole new life.

Shortly after closing the centre, I moved into a beautiful apartment in Illovo, which had been bought from the proceeds of the sale of my townhouse in Sandown. It was in an old building, so its proportions were generous compared to the average modern apartment, but it had been redecorated and equipped with all new furniture and fittings. There were new couches with exquisite and elegant coverings in different shades of pink, chairs in candy stripes of pinks and greens and rose-patterned curtains in every window. It used to have the most hideous carpets in every room, but these had been stripped away to reveal magnificent wooden floorboards. I adored my apartment and hoped the move would be the start of a new me. It was.

As Darren and I set about the drudgery of moving everything from the centre, once again I was grateful for my ability to dissociate. I felt nothing as we packed away eighteen months of work, some of it groundbreaking, some of it ordinary, all of it, I think, important. The centre had been a space for many remarkable addicts who burst into bloom after being with us for their treatment. Thankfully, Darren and I started talking again, after I sent him an SMS in which I took as much responsibility as I could at the time for my behaviour. I was relieved as our relationship started to improve.

Then just when it seemed things couldn't get any worse, one of our colleagues and dear friends died of a drug overdose. At this stage, I was so immersed in guilt and shame that I wanted to take blame for that tragedy too. Anna had been our first client and was a brilliant chef. After her treatment, we offered her a job. Her food was divine, as she put all her love into her cooking. She was like the heroine in the movie *Chocolat* and our food became renowned throughout the local recovery world. She and her husband Leon were like family, supporting us through everything up until the end. Anna was a hard-core addict and she and I shared many similar issues, but I believe that the eighteen months that she worked at One Life were some of the happiest in her life.

Then it was January 2008 and I was fourteen years clean, which should have been a time for great celebration, but this year's milestone felt decidedly different. I had never felt so alone. I reluctantly agreed to do the birthday thing at Narcotics Anonymous, but everything had changed. I was the Jezebel who in earlier times might have been burnt at the stakes. I feigned being okay, even owned the errors of my ways as I stood in front of them and shared what had been going on in my life over the past year. But underneath my platitudes and demure behaviour, I seethed with anger at what I perceived as a bunch of unfair hypocrites. I knew rationally that I was being paranoid and projecting my own feelings of guilt, and that not everyone was against me or judging me, but I wasn't well enough yet to feel this on an emotional level.

In February Darren and I went to see a psychic reader who, amongst other things, remarked, 'So when are you going to write your book?' I had thought about writing a book for years, but it had never gone further than that. The psychic's words were the encouragement I needed, and the next week I started writing. Paradoxically, this was also one of the most difficult times in my life, as writing this book forced me to face all my core fears on a level that pushed me beyond anything I had ever confronted. There were days when I felt so depressed I would have to make a commitment with myself to stay alive. Despite what I've said before about suicide no longer being an option because of my belief in reincarnation, I would plan how I was going to kill myself on the weekend right down to the last detail, and just thinking about it was enough to get me through another day. What stopped me from going through with it was Darren, and Mignon. I could not do this to Darren after everything he had been through, and Mignon would simply not survive without me.

I was drowning in fear, panic and nervousness, about everything in general and money in particular. There were times when I had no food in the apartment. For the first time in my life, I became extremely aware of prices and it was the biggest lesson in humility. But there was more to come. A little while later, having been somewhat behind with my repayments, my car was repossessed and I was forced to examine who I was without wheels. Initially I felt humiliated and ashamed, and when I walked down the road to the nearby shopping centre, I was convinced that passing motorists could see right through me and knew that I didn't have a car. It's amazing how much of my identity was hooked up in this. Heavy feelings of guilt and worthlessness had to be suffered and wrestled with and for a while I felt terribly sorry for myself, until there came the day when I suddenly 'got it'. After all the work I had done over the years, I knew deep within me that I was a worthwhile person and that this worth didn't depend on me having a car or any other external thing. But some of this understanding had been purely intellectual; what I was going through now was experiential, and I was able to stop feeling so attached. It was brilliant.

After that I became much more positive generally. Somehow all the other fears that had been lining up to frighten me dissipated, and I knew that I was going to be okay. Not having a car also allowed me the space to become more disciplined as far as writing was concerned. And I was blessed to have Ca, who schlepped me wherever I needed to go. In fact, we spent most days together, and we had such fun getting to know each other properly. I also got to spend quality time with my nieces, Janey and Suzie, which was great. If everything happens for a reason, then I do believe that part of my no-car status was about this very special time of bonding. My whole life I had been trying to escape my family and now in my fifties, I was discovering for the first time the pure delight of familial love.

Despite the financial adversity, I was beginning to enjoy the amount of time that I had available. I almost didn't know what to do with myself. Although I had gone back into private practice in early 2008, I was seeing only a few clients. Private practice suited me. It was calm and stress free. I liked it, had always liked it; it felt solid. Most of the clients who came to see me knew about what had happened at One Life, but chose to see me anyway. I was deeply touched by this.

I had been a workaholic for over ten years, and now I was constantly thinking, 'Oh, so is this what it feels like to have a life?' It felt gorgeously self-indulgent to read a book that I had had for years but which I simply had not had time for. Very slowly, I began to feel better, and my counselling shifted as I felt more enlivened and imaginative than I had in years.

A few months into the year, Darren announced that he was moving to Israel. I understood and applauded his decision. At the same time, of course, I felt a huge sense of loss. But he has settled down so well in the land of milk and honey and I have never heard him sound this happy before, which makes my heart sing. I know he needed to get away from here and perhaps specifically from me.

I have had to get used to not having him around to rely on, so it has been a huge growth experience for both of us.

I still had a lot of residual anger to deal with. There were people towards whom I felt a lot of resentment and bitterness, despite my earlier realisation that a lot of my feelings were the result of guilt and projection. But for the first time I actually allowed myself to experience true rage, rather than trying to repress it. When I mentioned this anger to Darren on the phone one day, he said, 'Well it's good that you're allowing yourself to release your feelings.' And then one day I stopped being angry. It was such a liberating sensation that I did a little skip around my lounge.

—

Today, as I write these final lines, I reflect on this journey that has been my life so far. I have gone through darkness and have been in the light of recovery, and, like so many others before me, what I have discovered is that the only thing that is real and transformative is love; everything else is an illusion.

I believe that I have earned the right to call myself a healer, albeit a wounded one, as I help to guide people through their own underworlds. Although I am ever vigilant for Ladymania, I can safely say that I am more content, more present than I have ever been. I feel like me, only better, and I'm drinking up these moments of what feels like real happiness.

I used to think that I would have plastic surgery on my arms to remove all evidence of my madness, but as I gaze down at my arms I feel quite loving towards my scars. I wear them well, and they glisten in the moonlight and let me know when the weather is about to change. They are my war wounds and, even though the fight is over, they are a reminder of endurance.

During all the trauma last year, I developed a new and unexpected addiction. I discovered house music. Playing Paul Oakenfeld or Roger Goode full blast was the only thing that quietened down all the shit in my head. I absolutely loved it. I still do. There is something about the sound that goes straight to my essence; as I melt into the pulsating beat, I feel sensual and female, and there is no sense of shame, only an awesome sense of how beautiful I feel exactly as I am.

The music is playing right now, filling my whole apartment with sound and as I whirl across the floor, Mignon whistles and bobs up and down and we give it all we've got to the sounds of DJ Tiesto's 'Do you feel me?'. I am so grateful to be alive. I continue to dance, freely now, but with feet firmly on the ground.

# Acknowledgements

I would like to thank the following people:

Darren Wasserman for being there and patiently reading all my chapters as I was writing them and for the excellent feedback.

Ca, Sid, Janey and Suzie Frankel for unconditionally supporting me through this process.

My editor Bronwyn McLennan for her ability to raise editing to another level of consciousness and helping to shape my manuscript to what it is today.

Louise Grantham from Penguin for making it happen and for always being present and available.

Reneé Naudé from Penguin for all her untiring help and support.

David Schröder from Penguin for being the first person to see my writing and for passing it on to the relevant people.

Kevin Standish, otherwise known as The Man, for all his years of dedication.

Dr Sheldon Zilesnick, otherwise known as Dr Wellness, for his commitment to my wellbeing and for being my miracle man.

Rabbi Mordecai Abraham for his unconditional caring and concern when I was at my lowest. I am forever grateful.

Evie Khumalo for many, many years of love and friendship and for making my life easier.

Greg Woolls for saving my life.

My clients for continuing to surprise, delight and enrich me.

Gil and Angelique Di Siena for years of beautiful hair, makeup and a special bond.